SketchUp to LayOut

The essential guide to creating construction documents

with SketchUp & LayOut

Written by: Matt Donley

SketchUp to LayOut
The essential guide to creating construction documents
with SketchUp & LayOut

Published by:
Bizfound, LLC
24 Michael Drive
Bristol, RI 02809
www.Bizfound.com

Ordering Information:
Visit www.SketchUptoLayOut.com for ordering information.

Credits:
Detail models by www.imiweb.org
Rendered image by Duane Kemp, www.KempPro.com

ISBN 978-0-9965393-0-2

masterSketchup.com

To my loving wife, Kelly

Contents

Introduction 1

How To Use This Book 6

Preparing Your Model for LayOut 11

Planning 11

Organization 18

Workflow Overview 29

Creating Scenes 32

Advanced Scenes for LayOut 36

Scene Anatomy 56

SketchUp Styles 62

Introduction

As a construction professional, you spend a lot of your time creating, designing, and building. You love how SketchUp helps you visualize your ideas in 3D. It's intuitive, fun, and easy to use, but at some point you'll need to share your ideas with others.

You need a way to create drawings on paper that communicate scale, dimensions, and clearly depict how to build your design.

This book is written specifically for architects, carpenters, woodworkers, and other construction professionals who want to use SketchUp Pro and LayOut to effectively communicate their 3D designs on paper.

Using SketchUp and LayOut together provides a complimentary set of tools for designing in 3D, then sharing your ideas in 2D.

What Will You Learn?

Before reading this book, you should already have some experience with SketchUp. This is not a beginners SketchUp book. We will be skipping over many of the fundamental skills you should already know how to do in SketchUp. If you are new to SketchUp, go to my website at www.MasterSketchUp.com to learn how to use SketchUp for free.

Building upon your basic knowledge of SketchUp, this book will show you how to properly prepare your models to be imported into LayOut.

Once you learn how to optimize your SketchUp models, you'll learn all about LayOut. You don't need any prior experience with LayOut to follow this book. You will become familiar with the user interface, and will learn how to insert SketchUp model viewports into your document. From there you will learn how to add dimensions and annotations to fully develop a set of construction documents.

Sample Projects

In order to help you understand the real world application for these concepts, I have included three example projects for you to follow along with. Download the book files at Sketchuptolayout. com/files. These projects will take the knowledge you've learned in the beginning of the book, and show you how to apply those skills in the real world.

Although these won't be step by step instructions, you will be able to see the general workflow used to create these projects so that you may apply the same workflow to your own projects.

By the end of this book, you will have the essential skills needed to use SketchUp & LayOut together to create completely annotated and dimensioned construction documents. Specifically, you will be able to do the following:

✓ Create annotated 2D construction documents in LayOut that can be printed out on paper to scale.

✓ Organize your SketchUp models in order to have complete control over the look of the viewports you create in LayOut.

✓ Customize your own SketchUp styles to create the exact look you want.

✓ Control lineweights of your model from LayOut.

✓ Maintain a dynamic link between SketchUp and LayOut in order to quickly propagate changes.

✓ Create custom titleblock templates for your drawings.

✓ Create section cuts and hatching in your models using numerous methods.

SketchUp Make vs SketchUp Pro

SketchUp is available in two versions; SketchUp Make, and SketchUp Pro. SketchUp Make is a free, fully functional 3D modeling software for personal use. SketchUp Pro is licensed for commercial use, has some additional features for professionals, and includes two add on programs called **LayOut** and **Style Builder**.

Besides being able to use SketchUp Pro for commercial use, these are some of the many additional features and benefits included in SketchUp Pro:

✓ Increased import/export capabilities

✓ Create interactive presentations

✓ Create construction drawings

✓ Print to scale

✓ Create dynamic components with custom attributes or behaviors

✓ Generate lists and reports

✓ Additional SketchUp tools: Solid modeling tools

✓ Create custom styles with Stylebuilder

✓ SketchUp Pro also has "Smart Labels", as well as the "Classifier", allowing you to attach metadata to your model components, such as IFC data.

To download SketchUp Make or SketchUp Pro, go to www. SketchUp.com

What is LayOut?

When you purchase SketchUp Pro, it comes bundled with another program called LayOut. LayOut is a companion program to SketchUp, meaning that they work in tandem with each other. LayOut cannot be purchased separately from SketchUp; you must purchase SketchUp Pro in order to get it.

The primary purpose of LayOut is to organize "viewports" of your SketchUp model onto digital "pages" so you can add annotations and dimensions to them and print them out to scale on paper and create presentations.

You can think of a viewport as a particular snapshot of your SketchUp model that is linked to a page in LayOut. Much like your word processor has digital pages for you to write on, LayOut has digital pages for you to arrange SketchUp viewports and add notes, dimensions, and titleblocks.

For the most part, you don't do any drawing or modeling in LayOut. You won't see many drawing tools in LayOut because it is expected that you will be doing all of your drawing in SketchUp.

The biggest advantage of using LayOut to create presentations is that your SketchUp models are dynamically linked to your LayOut document. If any changes are made to your model, you can update the model reference in LayOut and all the changes will update in your viewports.

LayOut 2015

This edition of the book has been updated for SketchUp Pro 2015. While most of the program features have remained the same, I have added content to cover all the new features.

With the introduction of SketchUp and LayOut 2015 came the first time we are seeing a 64-bit version. This means you should notice an increase of performance when working in SketchUp and

LayOut.

2015 also tied together a number of BIM features that have been building up over the years. This is the first time we are really seeing a cohesive approach to BIM modeling within SketchUp and LayOut. I've added an entire chapter on "BIM modeling" on page 71.

The biggest change to LayOut in 2015 were the additional Label tool features. I have added instructions on how to work with the new Label tool in the section named "Smart Labels", on page 153.

If you'd like to learn more about SketchUp & LayOut 2015, check out my article at www.mastersketchup.com/sketchup2015.

Style Builder

SketchUp styles allow you to change the visual properties of your model, giving your model a variety of unique appearances. You can make your model look hand drawn, painted, watercolor, or a number of other artistic formats.

The options are nearly endless when you have Style Builder, because you can actually create your own custom styles using this program. Specifically, Style Builder allows you to create custom edge profiles for use in your custom styles. Edges are but one of the parameters that make up a style.

This book is focused on SketchUp and LayOut, so we won't be talking about how to use Style Builder at all.

How To Use This Book

This book is organized into several parts that will serve to help you understand the overall workflow of a typical project while teaching you the specific steps to take in order to apply the principles to your own projects.

Preparing Your Model For LayOut

The first part of the book will help you create the right frame of mind for creating models specifically for LayOut. You will learn how to be efficient with your time by choosing the correct level of detail for your model.

You'll also learn proper model organizational methods to help you manage large models and control visibility of objects in your model. We'll take a close look at how scenes and styles work so you can completely customize the look of your model viewports.

After completing Part 1, you will know how to create SketchUp scenes optimized for LayOut.

LayOut Documents

We'll learn all about LayOut in this part of the book. We'll cover basics such as the user interface, toolbars, and tray panels, as well as familiarizing yourself with some of the basic tools and concepts of LayOut.

Once you've become familiar with the LayOut environment, we'll jump into some common tasks such as opening a new file and customizing a titleblock template, inserting SketchUp models, and adding annotations and dimensions. You'll also learn about how to create and reuse objects from your **Scrapbook panel**.

After creating a LayOut document, you'll learn about how to use the built-in presentation tools, as well as other export capabilities.

Advanced Techniques

At this point, you'll be able to complete your own construction documents using SketchUp and LayOut, but you might be looking for additional methods for creating section cuts or hatching.

This part of the book is all about different methods for preparing SketchUp scenes using custom materials, styles, and plugins. Use these tricks to further customize the look of your model viewports.

Table Project

Project files included with book: (Download at sketchuptolayout.com/files)

✓ **Table.skp**

✓ **Tablelayout.layout**

In this sample project, we walk through how to create a woodworking project in SketchUp, and the typical scenes that would be set up in order to export into LayOut.

You'll learn how to create exploded views and how to isolate different parts of your model in order to create custom views in LayOut.

Kitchen Project

Project files included with book: (Download at sketchuptolayout.com/files)

✓ **Kitchen.skp**

✓ **Kitchenlayout.layout**

This kitchen project will start by showing you some of the advantages of using pre-made components to save time while modeling.

In LayOut, you'll see examples of some advanced techniques including stacking viewports, and inserting section cut linework into your model.

House Project

Project files included with book: (Download at sketchuptolayout.com/files)

✓ **Farmhouse.skp**

✓ **Farmhouselayout.layout**

This sample project will walk you through the modeling and organizational process of building a house in SketchUp. This is a good example of why model organization is so important when working on large models.

You'll see many of the various hatching and section cut techniques in this project as well as viewport stacking.

Project Files

For the example projects explained in this book, the SketchUp and LayOut project files were included with the purchase of this book. By opening the files you'll be able to follow along in the chapter while exploring the project yourself. You can access the project files at sketchuptolayout.com/files.

You'll also be able to extract the custom styles, patterns, scrapbooks, and materials I used in the projects so you can use them in your own projects.

If you purchased the template package with this book, follow the instructions in the separate installation guide provided with the templates. If you did not purchase the template package, you can still purchase them by going to sketchuptolayout.com/bonuspacks.

Most of the work involved with creating a great LayOut document actually takes place inside SketchUp. Spending the time in SketchUp to prepare your model is the most important part of the process.

This part of the book is all about how to create models for the purpose of exporting them into LayOut. You'll learn specifically about model level of detail, organization, and how to leverage scenes and styles to create custom viewports for LayOut.

Planning

With a basic understanding of SketchUp, you can successfully create complex LayOut documents as long as you stay organized. Before you start modeling, you should review your project and determine the complete scope of work that you will be modeling.

TIP: In order to create a model for LayOut, you must have basic knowledge of SketchUp. If you've never used SketchUp before, or need a refresher, go to www.MasterSketchup.com/getting-started-with-trimble-SketchUp/ for a free course on learning the basics of SketchUp.

Level of Detail

Before you start modeling, you should have a rough idea as to how detailed your model needs to be. Having a good plan before you start modeling will save you time, keep you organized, and maintain consistency throughout your model.

The level of detail depends mainly upon the overall scope of the project, and the scale of the viewports you will be producing in LayOut.

Your model should be detailed just enough to communicate and coordinate your ideas clearly. A model with too much detail can add confusion, misinterpretation, and difficulty when modeling and when trying to work with viewports in LayOut.

High Level of Detail

For a long time, I had always drawn things in SketchUp exactly as they would be made in real life. **In other words, I would draw to a high level of detail in ALL of my models. (Figure 2-1)** But in most cases, this is a waste of time and will actually make it harder for you to model.

Figure 2-1
Creating models 100% accurate to real life is not the most efficient use of your time.

Each "part" of the cube is accurately modeled to within 1/16"

For example, if you look at an overall floor plan of a building, there is a relatively **low level of detail**. The level of detail is primarily determined by **what elements need to be dimensioned**. For the walls, you won't see each stud or the drywall or siding drawn in place, you'll just see an overall rectangular outline **representing** the wall.

But then, later on in the drawings you might get to a page showing all the wall type details. On this page, each element that makes up the wall needs to be identified and dimensioned so you would see a close up drawing with a **high level of detail** of the wall. You'll see the thickness of the stud, drywall, sheathing, siding, along with any vapor barriers and insulation.

Creating Detail Models

In many instances, you may find it makes sense to create separate "detail models" that represent typical assemblies in your project. (**Figure 2-2**) In the case of a house project, it could be a wall assembly, roof assembly, or door and window details. Over time, you can create a library of these detail models that you can reuse on different projects.

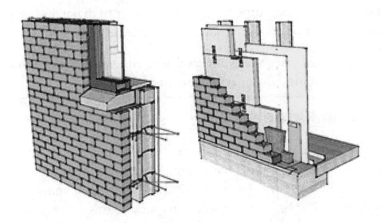

Figure 2-2
Separate detail models can be the source for your detail viewports. Credit: www. imiweb.org

Determining Level of Detail

Every job is different, so it's impossible to define a strict set of rules as to the level of detail you should draw. The level of detail of your model will vary greatly if you are creating construction drawings for an urban development, a house, an addition, a kitchen, or a woodworking project. Think of these three points before starting a new project to determine the level of detail required for the main model;

✓ What will be the largest viewport you'll need to capture, and at what scale will it be at on paper?

✓ As a rule of thumb, any details less than 1/8" on paper do not need to be modeled in your main model, and can be represented in a separate detail model or omitted altogether.

✓ If you only have a few details that you consider "detailed", you may alternatively decide to draw them in your main model, but place them on separate layers in order to isolate them in your viewports.

Types of Models

SketchUp is a visualization tool that can be used to create a number of different types of models. By categorizing your model based upon its final purpose, it becomes easier to make decisions about the level of detail you should be modeling at.

You should categorize your models as either **mock-up models, coordination models,** or **rendering models.**

Mock-up Models

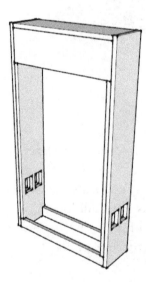

Figure 2-3
This mockup of a utility chase helped me visualize how it should be built in real life.

These types of models are created fast, with the main purpose of visualizing a problem and figuring out a solution quickly. This is the primary way I use SketchUp as a tool because I love how quickly it helps me visualize an assembly. (**Figure 2-3**)

You won't use layers or materials very much, this is a very basic functional model. Its context exists only in the space of the problem and the solution. The rest of the building or object is not modeled around it. You are only creating this model to figure out a specific detail. It's meant as a "throw away" model.

Once you've come up with your solution, you will refine the mock-up model into a coordination model.

Coordination Models

Coordination models are created for the **specific purpose of importing into LayOut**. They are not necessarily modeled to the exact physical shape of the objects they represent. Their primary purpose is to describe an object with just enough detail to clearly communicate what it represents and to provide points from which to attach dimensions to.

The **Farmhouse.skp** file included with this book uses basic shapes to represent the walls and floors to make it easier to dimension in LayOut, so it can be considered a coordination model. **(Figure 2-4)**

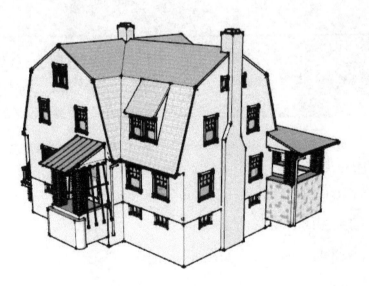

Figure 2-4 The **Farmhouse. skp** file included with this book is a good example of a coordination model.

A lower level of detail is used in order to create snap points that are easy to pull dimensions off of. Detailed models are created as separate models in order to communicate intricate details that appear typical in the project.

Rendering Models

A rendering model (**Figure 2-5**) is a model that is created to provide an artistic or photorealistic image or animation of the project. Renders can be simple perspective images exported directly from SketchUp, or they can be highly detailed images processed in a third-party rendering software.

Figure 2-5
This rendered scene was created from a SketchUp model designed specifically for rendering. Credit: Kemp Productions. www.KempPro. com

Some examples of rendering software that interface with SketchUp are:

✓ V-Ray - www.chaosgroup.com

✓ Shaderlight - www.artvps.com

✓ Twilight - www.twilightrender.com

✓ Lumion - www.lumion3d.com

✓ LumenRT - www.lumenrt.com

✓ Kerkythea - www.kerkythea.net

A model created for rendering has much more emphasis on photorealistic materials applied to the faces of the model. They will also have additional elements such as people, plants, furniture, and other objects to enhance the visual appeal of the render.

Multi-Purpose Models

It's important to understand the intended purpose of your model. By making a conscious decision about the type of model you are creating, you will maintain consistency and save time by only modeling what's important.

Most often, our SketchUp models actually serve more than one purpose. For instance, most small woodworking projects (chairs, tables, desks, etc.) can be created as one highly detailed model, using one file for mockup, coordination, and rendering.

When you use one model for multiple purposes, it becomes extra important to make sure you stay organized while modeling. You may need to create different versions of the same object; one that is optimized for coordination views, and one optimized for rendered views. Saving them on separate layers will enable you to hide whichever one you don't need at the moment.

By understanding that a model is serving multiple purposes, you will know how much detail you need to show, and how to organize your model layers in order to serve each purpose.

Chapter Summary

✓ Determine the level of detail before you start modeling.

✓ The three types of models are Mock-up Models, Coordination Models, and Rendering Models.

Organization

In this chapter, you'll learn how to organize your SketchUp model in a way that makes it easier to create scenes for LayOut. We won't go over any drawing techniques, as you should have at least some modeling experience with SketchUp before going into this chapter.

We'll be going over how to use groups and components to organize your model into logical containers, and how to assign them to layers in order to have complete control over the visibility of the objects in your model.

TIP Many of the examples in this chapter refer to the **Kitchen.skp** sample file included with your purchase of this book. Feel free to open up that model as you go through this chapter to see how the model is organized.

Figure 2-6 Use groups & components to organize the structure of your model.

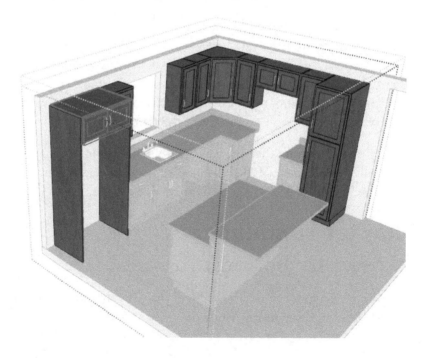

Groups & Components

Using groups and components in your model is critical to staying organized and maintaining the ability to edit objects in your model. Groups create an imaginary container around a collection of entities, protecting them from being affected by any entities or actions made outside of the group. (**Figure 2-6**)

Components are very similar to groups, except that each instance of a component is an exact replica of the other. (**Figure 2-7**) If any changes are made to one component, all copies of that component reflect those changes as well. Groups are independent from one another, meaning that once you've created a copy, you can edit one of them and the changes do not affect the other instances of that similar group. Each one is independent from the next.

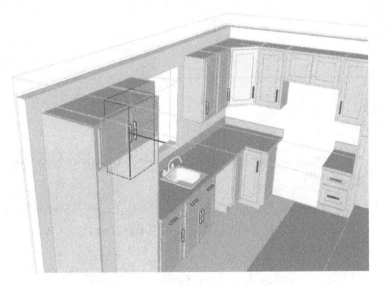

Figure 2-7
Components are great for identical objects that repeat throughout your model, like these cabinet pulls.

Step by Step

To create a group in SketchUp, follow these steps: (Figure 2-8)

1. Select all the entities you'd like to include in your group. (Triple-click with the **Select tool (Spacebar)** to select all connected entities.)

2. Right-click.

3. Select **Make Group**.

Figure 2-8
How to make a group from a selection of entities.

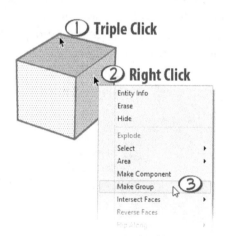

Step by Step

To create a component in SketchUp, follow these steps: (Figure 2-9)

1. Select all the entities you'd like to include in your component. (Triple-click with the **Select tool (Spacebar)** to select all connected entities.)

2. Right-click the selected entities.

3. Select **Make Component**.

4. In the window that pops up, type in a name for your component. Name it something that describes what the object is.

5. Click Create.

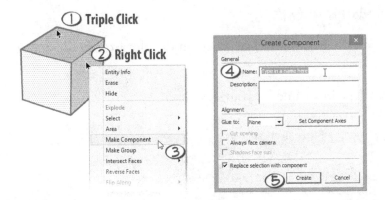

Figure 2-9
How to make
a component
from a selection
of entities.

TIP When creating new groups and components, you can include existing groups or components in them. You are not limited to selecting loose entities.

With groups and components, you can navigate the structure of your model using the **Outliner window**, located in **Window -> Outliner**.

In order to gain full control over the visibility of your model objects, you need to understand and use the functionality of layers.

SketchUp Layers

While groups and components organize the structure of your model, layers organize the visibility of your model. You must use layers if you want to be able to control object visibility when creating construction documents in LayOut. Layers allow you to hide specific objects and save their hidden state in scenes, which will then be imported into a LayOut viewport.

Step by Step

To create a new layer in SketchUp, follow these steps: (Figure 2-10) Go to **Window -> Layers** to make sure the **Layers window** is active.

1. In the **Layers window**, click on the plus icon to add a new layer.

2. Type in a name for your new layer.

Figure 2-10
How to add a new layer.

Step by Step

You can assign objects to layers by following these steps: (Figure 2-11) Go to **Window -> Entity Info** to make sure the **Entity Info window** is active.

1. Select the object(s) you'd like to assign to a layer.

2. The **Entity Info window** will show you information about the currently selected object(s), including its currently assigned layer.

3. To change the object's layer assignment, select a new layer from the drop-down menu.

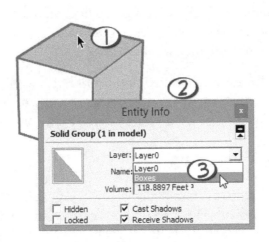

Figure 2-11
How to assign
objects to layers.

Layer0 is the default layer. It cannot be deleted. Although you are allowed to assign individual entities to layers, it's much better practice to keep all loose entities on the default **Layer0**, then create groups from those entities and assign those groups to a layer. (**Figure 2-12**)

This is because layers do not protect the structure of your model, they only affect visibility. So you could have some entities on a hidden layer but they could still be affected by changes in your model if they are not contained within a group or component.

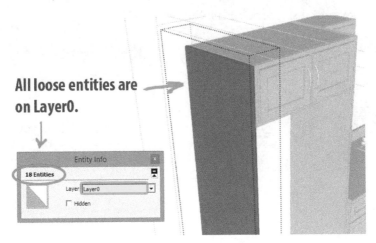

All loose entities are on Layer0.

Figure 2-12 All loose entities are assigned to the default **Layer0**. All layer assignments are done to groups or components.

By having everything inside a group or component and assigning them to layers, you can be sure that they won't be affected when hidden because they will be isolated.

You can create an unlimited number of layers within SketchUp. The key is to create a well thought-out set of layers designed specifically for the type of model you are working on.

Types of Layers

The layer structure for an architect will vary greatly from the layer structure of a woodworker, or carpenter. You may have many different types of layers in your model, but generally they will fall into one of the following categories:

✓ **Layer0** - This is the default layer in SketchUp. This should always be the active layer in your project. All loose entities should be assigned to **Layer0**.

✓ **Object Layers (MULTI)** - These are various layers that categorize the different types of objects in your model. In a kitchen, for example, you might have layers for wall cabinets, base cabinets, countertops, plumbing, etc. Basically, anything that you'll need to isolate on your construction documents should be on their own layer. These layers are assigned to groups of similar objects. (See **Figure 2-13**)

Figure 2-13
Examples of object layers.

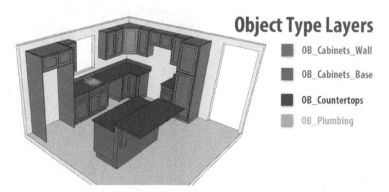

Object Type Layers

- ■ OB_Cabinets_Wall
- ■ OB_Cabinets_Base
- ■ **OB_Countertops**
- ■ OB_Plumbing

✓ **Phase/Location Layers (MULTI)** - Various layers that identify a specific phase, time, location, or stage of construction. For example: **Existing construction, Phase 1, Phase 2, Alternate 1, Alternate 2, Level 1, Level 2**, etc. Within phase/location groups, you may have many different object groups assigned to object layers. In the kitchen example, I have two location layers; **LO_Island** for the island, and **LO_Exterior Cabinets** for the exterior wall. (**Figure 2-14**)

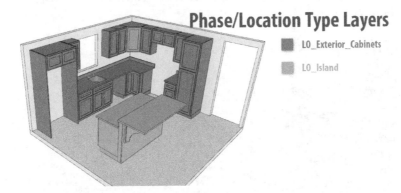

Phase/Location Type Layers

LO_Exterior_Cabinets

LO_Island

Figure 2-14
Examples of phase/location type layers

✓ **Scene Specific Layers (MULTI)** - Sometimes when creating a scene, you need to create special objects that are specific to that scene. Section cuts are a good example. You might create various layers that you only want visible when saving specific scenes.

You might have a different layer structure depending upon the type of project you are working on. The key is to have enough layers to easily manage object visibility in your model, but not too many where it causes confusion.

Objects on Multiple Layers

You'll notice in (**Figure 2-13**) and (**Figure 2-14**) there are objects that are assigned to more than one layer. You can do this by using groups and components to organize your model into multiple levels of organized collections, and assigning those groups to different layers. Explore the sample files to gain a better understanding as to how those objects are organized.

This offers you much greater control over the visibility of objects in your model. In (**Figure 2-15**), there's a kitchen island that consists of cabinets and countertops. The cabinet group is assigned to the **OB_Cabinets** layer and the countertop group is assigned to the **OB_Countertops** layer. Both of those groups are then included in another group, and it is assigned to the **LO_island** layer.

Figure 2-15
Organizing objects onto multiple layers using groups.

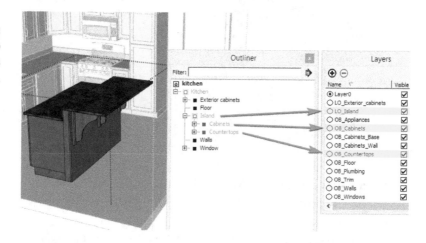

By organizing a model in this way, you have greater flexibility in how you hide objects. In this example, I can hide all the countertops in the model by hiding the **OB_countertop** layer, but I could alternatively hide only the island by hiding the **LO_Island** layer.

In (**Figure 2-16**), you can see all countertops are hidden by hiding the **OB_Countertop** layer. That's because all the countertops in the model are assigned to that layer, so when we hide it, all the countertops become hidden.

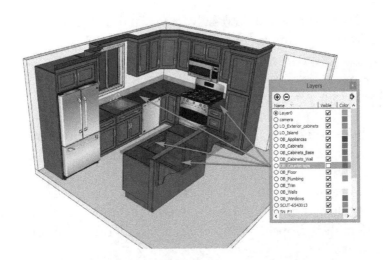

Figure 2-16
Hide countertops by disabling the **OB_Countertop** layer.

If you want to hide everything in the island, you just hide the layer **LO_island**. (**Figure 2-17**) Even though the countertops and cabinets are within their object specific layer groups, both the cabinets and the countertops have been placed inside another group representing the entire island. That master group encompassing the entire island is assigned to the layer **LO_island**. When you hide that master layer, all objects within the group will hide too, even if they are also assigned to other layers that are still active.

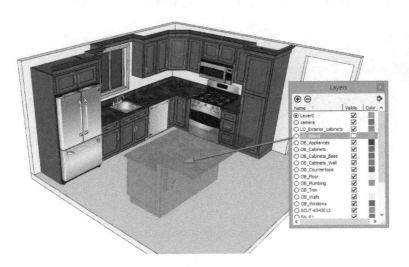

Figure 2-17
Hide the entire island by disabling the **LO_Island** layer.

Don't worry if you don't fully understand this concept just yet. We will go into greater detail on how this works and how to implement this in the sample project chapters.

Chapter Summary

It is never too early or too late to begin organizing your model. However, you should never let model organization get in the way of your creative process. At certain points during modeling, you should pause and review the structure of your model. Make sure absolutely everything is within a group or component, and assign them to their proper layers so you can control the visibility of those elements.

✓ Determine the level of detail of your model before you begin, in order to maintain consistency and save time during modeling.

✓ Categorize your model as either a mock-up model, coordination model, or rendering model, or a combination of models in order to understand how you should draw and organize it.

✓ Use groups and components to organize the structure of your model.

✓ Use layers to control the visibility of your model by assigning layers to groups and components you've created.

✓ Use external reference models to break up your project into smaller files and separate the organization of scenes.

Workflow Overview

SketchUp and LayOut work hand in hand with each other. Before we start diving into the details on how to create construction documents, let's look at a general overview of the complete process.

SketchUp

1. Before you start building your model, identify the specific views you'd like to show in your LayOut document. This will help you decide whether or not you'd like to create separate detail models for some of the viewports.

2. Build your model, keeping in mind the level of detail required for the views you thought of in the previous step. Assign loose entities to groups/components. Group similar objects together and assign them to their appropriate object type layer. Also, assign groups and layers to objects according to their phasing or location. Visualize what you want the final viewport to look like to make sure you are isolating the proper objects.

3. Once you've created your model, start creating scenes for the different perspectives you'd like to import to LayOut viewports.

LayOut

When you're done modeling in SketchUp, you'll create a new document in LayOut. Then, you can begin inserting your model into various viewports.

1. Open a new LayOut document. Use a template with your preferred settings and styles.

2. Import model viewports onto pages in LayOut. **Set the viewports to the scenes you created in SketchUp.**

3. Position and re-size the viewports to where you want them on the pages. Set the scale of the viewport models.

4. Add dimensions and annotations.

5. If changes are needed, make them in the SketchUp model. Update the model reference in LayOut to automatically show the changes throughout the document.

Objects to Draw in LayOut

As a rule of thumb, any representation of a physical object should be drawn in SketchUp. In fact, you should try to do all of your "drawing" in SketchUp, and leave things like dimensions and annotations to be created in LayOut.

Here are some ideas for objects that should be created in LayOut:

✓ **Dimensions** - Do not use the **Dimension tool** in SketchUp. LayOut's dimension tools are much more robust, and you have more control over the scale of the text.

✓ **Annotations/Leaders**- All text should be created in LayOut to ensure proper scale to the page size and to retain more control over the format.

✓ **Symbols** - Drafting symbols should be applied in LayOut by using pre-made elements from your Scrapbook.

✓ **Titleblock Elements** - One of LayOut's primary features is its ability to create properly scaled pages with built in titleblocks.

Chapter Summary

✓ Create your model first in SketchUp, then import various scenes of your model into LayOut viewports and add dimensions and annotations.

✓ Draw all representations of physical objects in SketchUp and all dimensions and annotations in LayOut.

Creating Scenes

When you insert a model viewport into LayOut, you have the ability to manipulate the model using a number of standard views. You can also assign whichever style you want to the model, right from LayOut. You can even double-click on the model to enter "model space" and orbit the camera around to get the exact view you want.

Although it seems really convenient to be able to do this right from LayOut, I only recommend doing this for basic perspective views of models.

Most viewports in LayOut should be set to scenes that have been carefully prepared in SketchUp ahead of time.

Creating your scenes ahead of time inside SketchUp will give you much greater control over the look of your model and will make it easier to share settings between scenes.

Creating a New Scene

Step by Step

To create a new scene, follow these steps: Go to **Window -> Scenes** to open the **Scenes window**. (**Figure 2-18**)

1. Configure your model as to how you'd like to save the scene by orienting the camera, hiding layers, selecting a style, etc.

2. To save a new scene, click the plus sign in the **Scenes window**.

3. Rename the scene to something that is representative to the contents of the scene.

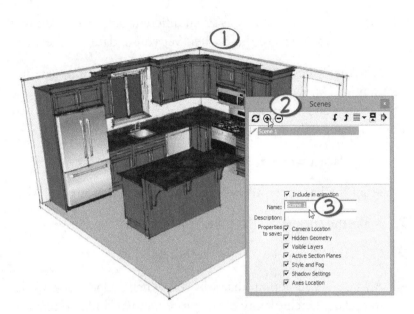

Figure 2-18
How to add a
new scene to
your SketchUp
model.

You'll notice that SketchUp adds a tab strip above the workspace window that allows you to easily recall the scene. In the **Scenes window**, you can change the name of the scene to something more relevant. It's good to name scenes by the name of the elevation, or something else that will be easier to remember when you are recalling the scene from inside LayOut.

You'll also see all of the properties that the particular scene is remembering. If there's a check mark next to the property, SketchUp will remember its state when the scene was last created or updated. If it is not checked, SketchUp will not make any changes to that property when you recall the scene. We will go into much more detail on what each of these properties mean in the chapter on Scene Anatomy.

Updating a Scene

Whenever you want to make an update to a scene, you have to tell SketchUp which of the properties you want to update. Since each scene can have as many as seven different properties, you may not want to update all of them whenever you update a scene.

It is usually best to activate a scene first, before you update it, that way you know all of the properties match what was saved last under that scene. From there, you make changes to only what you want to change, then you update it.

To update a scene, follow these steps: (Figure 2-19)

1. From the **Scenes window**, select the scene you want to update.

2. Make the changes to the properties you want to change.

3. Click the update icon in the **Scenes window**.

4. A window will pop up that asks you which properties you'd like to update. Uncheck any of the properties you'd like to remain unchanged.

5. Click Update.

Figure 2-19
How to update a scene.

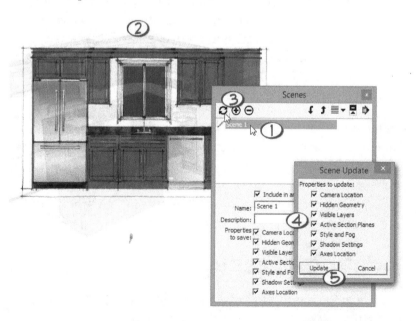

Navigating Scenes

In SketchUp, you can recall any scene by clicking on the proper tab above the modeling workspace. You can also navigate the scenes from the **Scenes window**. (**Figure 2-20**)

You can change the view inside the **Scenes window** from the drop down menu to display thumbnails of the scenes, or to list them by name.

To change the order in which they are displayed, select a scene in the **Scenes window**, then click the move up or move down button.

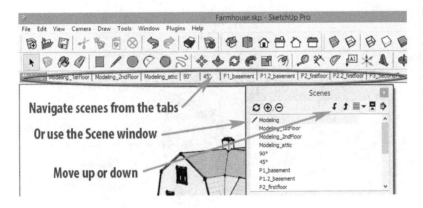

Figure 2-20
Navigate scenes from the tabs above the workspace or from the **Scenes window**.

Chapter Summary

✓ Scenes are important to the process of exporting models to LayOut because they can be assigned to viewports.

✓ You can update specific scenes properties after you've created them, without resetting all of the original properties.

✓ Navigate scenes from the scene tabs, or from the **Scenes window**.

Advanced Scenes for LayOut

Aside from creating simple scenes by orienting your camera and selecting a style, you can create complex scenes from your model to extract the exact information you want to show in your LayOut document.

There are **five distinct areas** you have control over when saving scenes. Refer to (**Figure 2-21**) for a graphic representation of these five parts in relation to your SketchUp workspace.

Figure 2-21 The five parts of a scene graphically represented in context with your computer monitor.

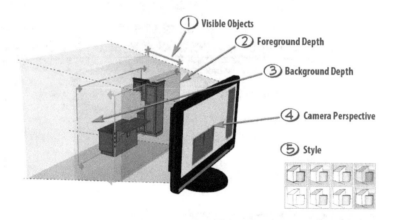

1. **Visible Objects** - Controlled by hiding/unhiding layers, but also includes visibility of other objects like section planes, guides, etc.

2. **Foreground Depth (Optional)** - The viewing plane at which you begin to see objects in your scene. By default, the foreground depth starts at the location of your camera, but you can manually set a foreground depth using section cuts and clipping planes.

3. **Background Depth (Optional)** - How deep into your model

do you want to see objects? If there are objects that you want to hide from the background view of your scene, you can obscure them from view using object masks or fog. In most scenes, however, you'll be able to hide objects by simply hiding their layers, so defining a background depth isn't always necessary.

4. **Camera perspective & settings** - Includes location of camera, field of view, and perspective settings.

5. **Style** - Determines how your model will look. This includes render settings for the faces and edges in your model, but also includes specialty settings like watermarks, guides, and section planes.

You don't need to define all five of these in every scene you create for LayOut. Foreground depth and background depth are optional, and they depend upon what you want your scene to look like.

Visible Objects

When creating scenes, you have the ability to control the visibility of anything in your model **as long as you have taken the time to organize your model properly using layers.** In simple models, you might make everything in your model visible in every scene. But in complex models you might decide to create scenes that only show certain parts of your model. (**Figure 2-22**)

Figure 2-22
Control the visible objects in your scene by hiding layers. Here, the **OB_Appliances, OB_Trim**, and **OB_Window** layers are hidden.

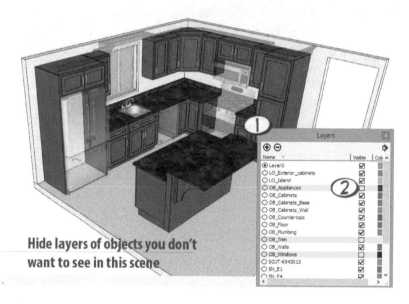

Hide layers of objects you don't want to see in this scene

Layers

Step by Step

To control the visibility of objects in your model, you need to hide the layers that you don't want to see in your scene. **To hide layers in your model, follow these steps: (Figure 2-22)**

1. Go to **Window -> Layers** and make sure the **Layers window** is active.

2. Uncheck the boxes in the column labeled "visible" for layers that you'd like to hide from your scene.

Foreground Depth

By default, the foreground depth of your scene starts at the position of your camera (**Figure 2-23**). Naturally, you won't see any objects that are behind your camera.

If you want to define a foreground depth that is independent from your camera location, you need to use some type of section cut. There are a couple of different ways to create section cuts in your model.

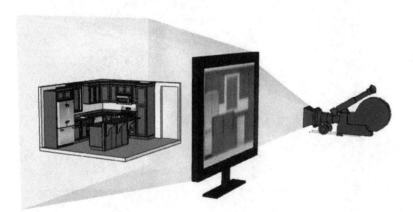

Figure 2-23
Think of your computer monitor as the "lens" of your camera. By default, the position of your camera defines your foreground depth.

With a section cut or a clipping plane, you can set a foreground depth manually, and have the ability to zoom your camera to any scale you want without affecting the foreground depth of the scene.

Section Planes

SketchUp has a special object, called a section plane, that can temporarily "slice" through your model to create a section cut view. Section plane objects are non-destructive, so they don't affect your model entities at all. They don't literally cut your model, they just create a visibility plane that

Figure 2-24 Section Plane object icon

lets you peer inside.

When you insert a section plane object into your model, a visual plane will appear in your model. That plane will have four arrows, one at each corner, pointing in the direction of the cutting view. You have the ability to make a section plane active or inactive, and you can also hide the section plane object itself.

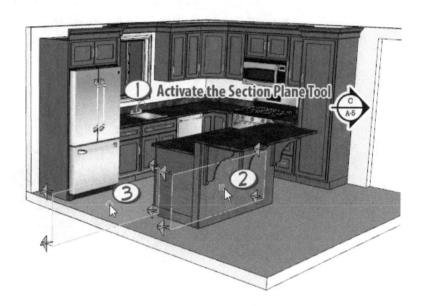

Step by Step

To insert a section plane, follow these steps: (Figure 2-25)

1. Activate the **Section Plane tool** located in the Tool menu, or by clicking the Section Plane icon.

2. Hover over a surface in your model that is on the same plane as the one you wish your section cut to be on. Hold the **SHIFT** key to lock reference to that plane.

3. Move the section plane object to the place where you'd like the cut to be. Click to place the section plane object.

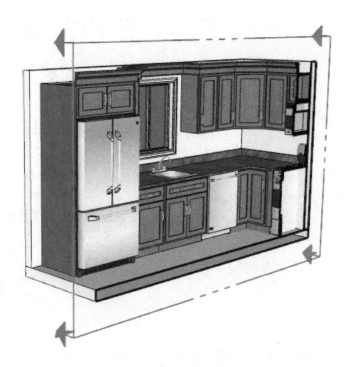

Figure 2-26
Completed
section plane
object insertion.

(**Figure 2-26**) shows a completed, active section plane.

You can manipulate a section plane object with the **Move (M) and Rotate (Q) tool** (**Figure 2-28**). You can also make copies of them or place them within groups, components, or assign them to layers. To reverse the viewing direction of a section plane object, right-click it and select "reverse".

Notice how section cuts expose the unsightly interior of your model? There are various ways to make the section cut look much better. We'll look at numerous ways to do that in the section, Advanced Techniques.

Figure 2-27
Section plane objects can be manipulated and organized like other objects in your model.

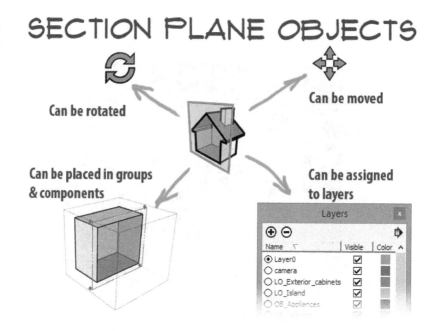

New section plane objects will automatically become the active cutting plane. They will also un-hide all section plane objects in your model. There can only be one active section plane at a time, unless they exist within different groups or components.

In any given model you are bound to have many different section planes located throughout. They will tend to clutter your workspace if you don't manage them well enough. SketchUp provides two special toggle buttons specifically for section planes so you don't have to introduce any additional procedure into your current modeling workflow to control their visibility.

In most of your scenes, you'll want to hide the section plane object from view, leaving only the resulting section cut. If you go to **View -> Section Planes**, you can toggle all the section planes in your model to be hidden or visible. It is also nice to hide them while you're modeling to reduce visual clutter. The only time you really need them turned on is when you are adding a new one, manipulating, or removing an existing one.

TIP While modeling, use a style that hides all section plane objects so you don't have to constantly toggle the button.

Besides manually controlling each active section plane, you also have the ability to turn off all section cuts in your model. **View -> Section Cuts** will toggle all section cuts either on or off.

When saving a scene with a section cut, you'll want to make sure the scene saves the "Active Section Planes". You'll then temporarily turn on the section plane object visibility so you can find the plane you want to activate. Right-click on that section plane object and select "Active Cut".

TIP If you want the camera perspective to be aligned perfectly with the section plane, right-click on it and select "Align View".

Section plane visibility and section cut visibility are two separate properties that can be saved within styles. If you are creating a style for scenes that will be used in LayOut, make sure you turn off section plane object visibility, but turn on section cut visibility. Otherwise, you'll notice your section planes will keep reappearing every time you change scenes.

Clipping Planes

If you don't want to have to keep track of and organize section planes throughout your model, you can insert a clipping plane using the **Position Camera tool** to set foreground depth.

The advantage of using the **Position Camera tool** is that clipping planes are not inserted as objects, but are simply remembered as a camera setting when you save the scene.

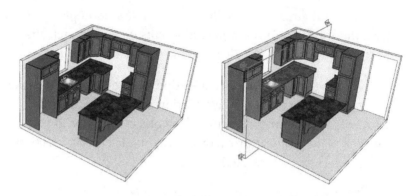

CLIPPING PLANE **VS** SECTION CUT

Clipping planes will only work in **Parallel Projection Camera** mode. It will also apply the clipping plane to the entire model, instead of being able to limit the section cut to a group or component like a section plane object can. But for creating overall orthogonal viewports, this is a really handy method.

Step by Step

To create a clipping plane at a specified depth in your model, follow these steps:

1. In SketchUp, go to the Camera menu and make sure "Parallel Projection" is selected.

2. To activate the **Position Camera tool**, go to the **Camera -> Position Camera**.

   TIP Before using the **Position Camera tool**, orbit so that you are about 45° off alignment to the direction you'd like the plane to face.

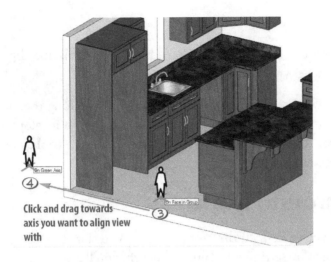

Figure 2-29 With the Position Camera tool, click and drag to pick a point for the clipping plane and to align the view

Click and drag towards axis you want to align view with

3. Click and hold at the point where you'd like the foreground depth to start. (**Figure 2-29**)

4. Drag your mouse towards the direction of your scene content. You can lock to an axis or snap to points in your model in order to align the view.

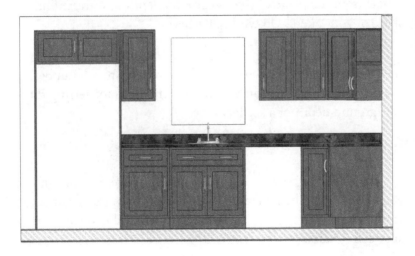

Figure 2-30 The aligned camera perspective after using the Position Camera tool.

You should now have a cut away view of your model, identical to the view a section plane would have rendered. (**Figure 2-30**) But with this method, you don't have to deal with the section plane object in your model.

Just save this in a scene, and you'll be able to recall this clipping plane whenever you activate that scene.

TIP If you are trying to create a clipping plane along the blue axis, you must first align the view perpendicular to it (along the green or red axis). Then, use the **Position Camera tool** again along the blue axis.

Background Depth

Once you've defined the point at which you start to see objects in your scene by setting a foreground depth, you'll also need to figure out the point at which you want to stop seeing objects by defining a background depth.

In some models, you may not need to define a background depth. You might be able to control the visible objects in your scene simply by using layers. Or, you might want to see your entire model from the plane of the foreground depth into the infinite space of your SketchUp workspace beyond.

Yet in other models, you might need to limit the depth of the scene but you can't achieve the look you desire by simply hiding layers. Here are some additional methods for setting the background depth of a scene.

Fog

Fog is an easy way to remove objects from the background of your scene. It gradually fades your scene out into the distance and you have complete control over the position of the fog and the rate at which it fades.

Getting the correct fog depth involves playing around with the sliders and visually checking to see which objects disappear.

To insert fog into your model to define a fading background depth, follow these steps: (Figure 2-31) Open the **Fog window** in SketchUp by going to **Window -> Fog.**

Step by Step

1. Turn on fog by checking the "Display Fog" box.

2. Set the depth at which you want fog to start by adjusting the left slider.

3. Set the point at which you want all objects to be hidden by adjusting the right slider.

Everything to the left of the first slider will be 100% visible. Everything between the two sliders will gradually fade into the background. Everything to the right of the last slider will be completely hidden.

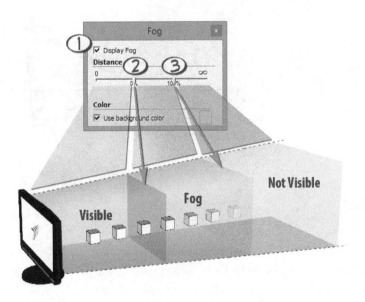

Figure 2-31 Fog allows you to set two points at which objects will fade into the background.

One of the disadvantages of using fog to control scene depth is that it won't work if you set your viewport to **Vector** mode in LayOut. (We will talk about what this means in a later chapter.) You will only be able to use this method if you know you will be rendering the viewport in **Raster** or **Hybrid** mode in LayOut.

TIP Fog will not hide edges when using a style that is using a custom edge style. Instead, the materials on faces will only be affected.

Section Cut Sandwich

You can use a section plane object pointing towards the camera in order to define a cutting plane at the exact depth where you want to cut off your scene content (**Figure 2-32**).

Figure 2-32 Use two section cuts facing each other to control foreground and background depth.

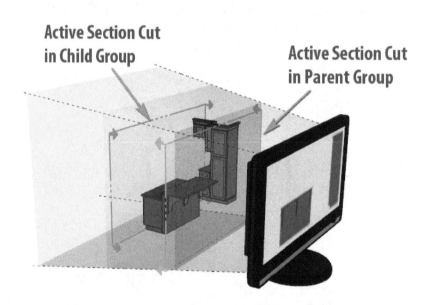

Active Section Cut in Child Group

Active Section Cut in Parent Group

In order to do this, you need to make sure you place this section plane object in a different group because SketchUp will only allow one active cutting plane per context.

Object Masking

Another way to control the background depth of a SketchUp scene is by creating an object mask. An object mask is a method in which you block the visibility of objects in your model by creating a large rectangle that expands past the field of view of the particular scene.

To create an object mask, follow these steps: (Figure 2-33)

1. Draw a large rectangle with the **Rectangle tool (R)**, and locate it where you want to block the view of certain objects. Make sure you extend the rectangle beyond the view of the camera or hide its edges.

2. Orient the camera so that you can see the objects in front of the object mask.

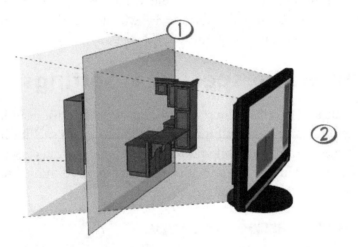

Figure 2-33 An object mask needs to extend past the view of the camera or have hidden edges.

There's nothing special about an object mask. It is literally just a rectangle with a material applied to it that is identical to the background color of the style. (Should be white to match the color of paper in LayOut.) By doing this, it creates the **illusion** that the surface of the object mask is actually the background of the model.

Since most object masks are applicable to specific scenes, you may want to create a special layer to assign them to.

✓ Because they are actual SketchUp objects, you have great

control over the positioning of the object when compared to the adjustment capabilities of fog.

✓ You can also create complex shapes that only block certain objects, but let others show. Hide the edges of the shape if they extend into the view of the camera.

✓ Create multiple custom shaped object masks positioned at different depths to have complete control over complex scenes.

✓ Object masks create a great effect when combined with the X-ray style. Anything behind the mask will appear as dotted lines, while anything in front of the mask will appear normally.

✓ Be aware that you won't be able to stack viewports using this method, because the object mask will also block any viewports underneath it in LayOut.

Camera Perspective & Settings

Instead of selecting a standard camera perspective from inside LayOut, you can save all the camera settings in a scene. In the simplest terms, you orbit and zoom the camera to the view you'd like to have in the viewport. But there are some additional settings you can define with your scene as well.

Camera Perspective Type

By default, you model in **perspective** mode. Perspective mode is similar to how you see things in real life. Things that are closer to you look bigger, and things that are farther away look smaller.

Because of this, the view becomes slightly distorted. Notice how the outside edges of each table leg look out of plumb. (**Figure 2-34**) In reality, its the inside edges that are tapered. Perspective mode creates this illusion.

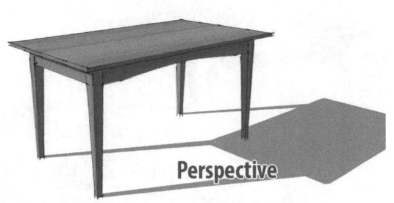

Figure 2-34
Perspective mode is a great camera setting for modeling and for creating off-angle scenes.

In **parallel projection,** also called "orthographic mode", all objects are scaled uniformly, so they do not get smaller if they are further away from the camera, but retain the same scale no matter where they are placed in the depth of the view. (**Figure 2-35**) Since everything is at a fixed scale in parallel projection mode, it's possible to assign an absolute scale to scenes set in this projection mode.

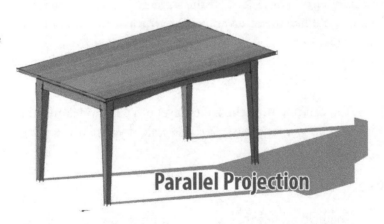

Figure 2-35
Parallel Projection does not distort the model with depth, and is great for adding dimensions to.

Two-point perspective mode has two vanishing points, and all vertical edges remain parallel with each other. (**Figure 2-36**)

Figure 2-36 Two-Point Perspective reduces camera distortion and keeps lines vertical.

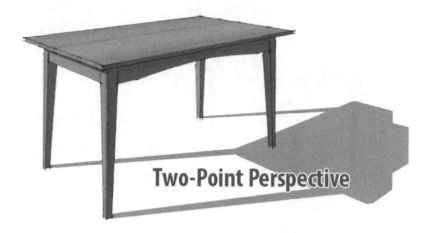

Figure 2-36 Two-Point Perspective reduces camera distortion and keeps lines vertical.

To change your camera settings, go to the Camera menu and select either Parallel Projection, Perspective, or Two-Point Perspective.

Zoom Level

Before saving the camera location property to a scene, you should set the zoom level of the scene to the approximate scale you would like to see when you insert the scene into a LayOut viewport. Doing this will make it easier for you to position the viewport contents and to help identify the precise scale at which you should display the viewport.

You can fine tune the zoom level of your model once in LayOut, as well as define a precise scale if you're using parallel projection.

Field of View

The field of view basically determines how much of your model will fit into the viewable area. If you have a wide field of view angle, you will see more of your model. If you have a smaller field of view, you will see less of it.

To change the field of view, go to the Camera menu, select Field of View, then type in a new value and press enter.

Just keep in mind that as you create a wider field of view, you introduce more distortion into the view. (**Figure 2-37**)

Figure 2-37
The field of view affects how much of your model fits within the view, but it also affects lens distortion.

Styles

Styles are what define how your model will look. You can change how your edges and faces look, define a background, watermarks, as well as many other specialty settings. (**Figure 2-38**)

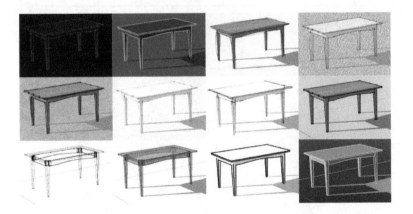

Figure 2-38
Examples of various styles built in to SketchUp that you can use to change how your model looks.

Styles are applied to the entire model, so you can only have one style active at a time. If you want to create a viewport that shows objects with different styles, you'll need to isolate those objects onto their own scene, and apply a different style to them.

To change the style of your SketchUp model, follow these steps: Open the Styles window by going to Window -> Styles.

1. Under the select tab, open a folder from the drop down menu.

2. Click on a style to activate it.

Figure 2-39
Change the style
from the **Styles**
window.

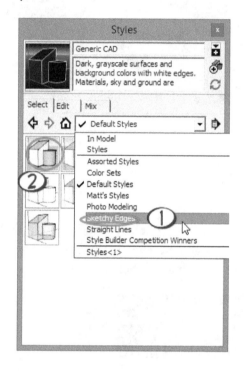

Chapter Summary

✓ There are five distinct areas of a SketchUp scene created for LayOut: Visible objects, foreground depth, background depth, camera perspective, and style.

✓ Foreground depth can be defined using the camera position, a section plane or the **Position Camera tool**.

✓ Background depth can be defined by using fog, a section cut, or object masking.

✓ Camera perspective is controlled by orbiting and zooming the camera to the position you want, then selecting a camera perspective type.

✓ Zoom level should be set to the relative scale you'd like to see in the LayOut viewport.

✓ Styles control the overall look of your model.

Scene Anatomy

Scenes allow you to save snapshots of your model. They are very powerful because they also allow you to save configurations of various attributes of your SketchUp model. You can access the **Scenes window** by going to **Window -> Scenes (Figure 2-40).**

Figure 2-40 The **Scenes window**

Scenes allow you to save the following attributes of your model:

✓ Camera Location

✓ Hidden Geometry

✓ Visible Layers

✓ Active Section Planes

✓ Style and Fog

✓ Shadow Settings

✓ Axes Location

Visualizing Scene Properties

One of the major properties scenes save is object visibility. You use layers to organize object visibility. Groups and components are used to organize object structure. To fully understand this concept, and how all the other properties of a scene relate, see (**Figure 2-41**)

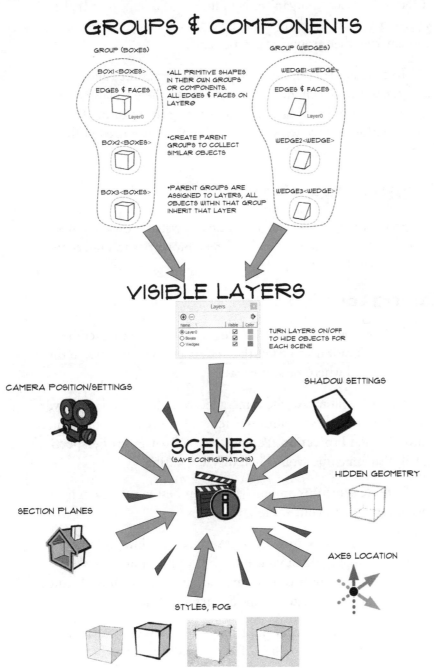

Figure 2-41
SketchUp
organizational
chart.

The core "parts & pieces" of a SketchUp model are edges and surfaces. In order to organize them into logical objects to make selection and manipulation easier we place them into invisible containers; either groups or components.

To control the visibility of all the different groups and components in our model we need to assign them to layers. By setting the visibility of each layer and saving the resulting layer configuration in a scene, we can recall those customized visibility states very easily.

Scene Properties

Scenes can save a number of different visual properties of a model. Let's take a look at each of these properties to understand exactly what they do.

Camera Location

This setting is used in most scenes. A scene that remembers the camera location will orbit the camera perspective back to the location it had when the scene was last saved.

Not only will it save the camera location, but it will also save all the camera settings as well. It will remember if you had the camera set to **Parallel Projection, Perspective,** or **Two-Point Perspective**. It will also remember your **Field of View** setting.

Here are some tips on how you might best use the camera location setting in your scenes.

✓ Saving camera location in your scenes will allow you to export a video animation of your model. If you want to exclude a specific scene from your animation, uncheck the box "Include in Animation" located in the **Scenes window**.

✓ While working in your model, it is usually best to turn off animation between scenes. This will save you a ton of time. Go to **Window -> Model Info** and click on **Animation**. Disable the "Enable scene transitions" check box.

✓ Save a scene in perspective mode and zoom out so you can see all of your model. It's a great shortcut if you ever get lost in your model, you can just click on this default scene to bring you back out.

✓ When you want to get a wide angle view of a room, go to **Camera -> Field of View,** and set it to a higher value like 70.

The Camera Location setting is essential for setting up scenes for LayOut. By saving a specified perspective of your model, you will be able to place that exact perspective right into your LayOut document in a viewport.

Hidden Geometry

This setting is a little confusing because it only refers to geometry, groups, and components not existing within any other groups or components. It will not save the visibility state of any objects that are nested within any group or component.

The bottom line is that when trying to control visibility of objects, you should be assigning them to layers and turning those layers on and off as needed before saving the scene.

Visible Layers

By assigning groups and components to different layers, you can control the visibility of many objects at once by turning layers on and off.

Because scenes have the capability to remember which layers are on or off, this is the primary way you should be controlling visibility in your viewports.

Active Section Planes

If you are using section planes to expose cut away views of your model, you are likely to have a number of section planes in your model at the same time. But you will only want certain ones active in any particular scene.

Scenes can remember which section planes are active by enabling this setting.

Style and Fog

This setting lets you save any of the style parameters, including background, sky, edge style, face style, etc. These settings are what give your models a unique visual style.

Some styles can create things like wireframe models, or beautiful sketchy styles to bring into LayOut. Using fog can help you control scene background depth.

Shadow Settings

Control all of your shadow settings separately from your style settings. Shadow settings allow you to create realistic shadows by geo-locating your model and selecting a moment in time so SketchUp can accurately model the sun position above your model.

The axes location and orientation are what provide the 3-axis references for the SketchUp inference system. By setting up a scene with different axes locations, you can quickly switch back and forth between commonly used orientations.

Selective Memory

It's worth noting that you are not forced to have your scene "remember" all of these properties; You can specify only the ones you want the scene to remember.

For instance, let's say you want to create a scene that brings your camera back to a specific location, but you don't want the scene to change the visibility of the layers you happen to be working on at the moment. By unchecking the "Visible Layers" option, that scene won't pay attention to layers when you active it.

Chapter Summary

✓ Use scenes to create views of your SketchUp model that you want to export to LayOut.

✓ You can choose which attributes each scene remembers.

✓ You can choose which attributes are updated when you update a scene.

✓ Name your scenes so they can be identified easily.

SketchUp Styles

Styles are the powerhouse behind what makes SketchUp so unique. They control every aspect of what you see in the SketchUp workspace, exports, and viewports in LayOut.

To access the **Styles window** in SketchUp, go to **Window -> Styles**. With the **Select tab** active, click on any of the pre-made styles to see how they change the look of your model. (**Figure 2-42**) Click the drop down menu to explore many more folders of styles.

Figure 2-42
Change the style from the **Styles window**.

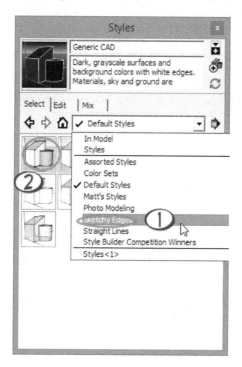

To understand exactly what gets saved in a SketchUp style, click on the **Edit tab**.

Edge Settings

Under edge settings, you can activate or deactivate Edges, Back Edges, Profiles, Depth Cue, Extension, Endpoints, and Jitter. You also have the ability to define the size of some of those attributes. (**Figure 2-43**)

If you are editing a style that has been created with Style Builder, you will see a different screen. You will see most of the same options with the exception of endpoints. The "Halo" setting will be in its place, and you will have a slider that will affect the level of detail of the edge stroke.

You can also change the color of the edges to either match the color of each object's material, or to color by axis. You can't manually assign different colors to different edges, you must apply these settings to your entire model globally.

Figure 2-43
Edges settings in the **Styles window**.

The best way to discover how these settings affect your model is to play around with them yourself, but here are some tips for using Edge Settings:

✓ **Back Edges** will reveal all edges within your model, but if they are obstructed from view by a face they will appear as a faint dashed line.

✓ **Color by axis** is a great way to examine your model to confirm that all of your edges are parallel with the proper axis. Realigning your axis will let you confirm edges that may have been drawn on a different angle.

Face Settings

These settings will affect how the surfaces within your model will look. You will notice the effects of these settings best when you assign textured materials to your models. (**Figure 2-44**)

Figure 2-44
Face settings
in the **Styles**
window.

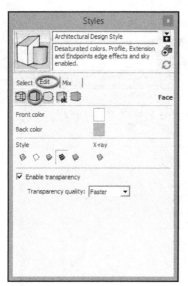

First, you can set the colors of your default faces. Since every face has a front and a back, they give you two selections to make. I really wouldn't change these, since it is a good idea to standardize the default face colors so you can readily identify if a face has a material applied to it or not, regardless of which style you have active.

The different face styles are **wireframe**, **hidden line**, **shaded**, **shaded using textures**, and **shaded using all same**. **Xray mode** will make all of the faces semi-transparent no matter which face style is selected.

You can also toggle whether you want transparent materials to be enabled or disabled.

Background Settings

Some styles have a different colored "sky" and "ground". In situations where you are creating scenes for LayOut, you will almost always want to have a white background. This will make sure the background matches the page background in LayOut.(**Figure 2-45**)

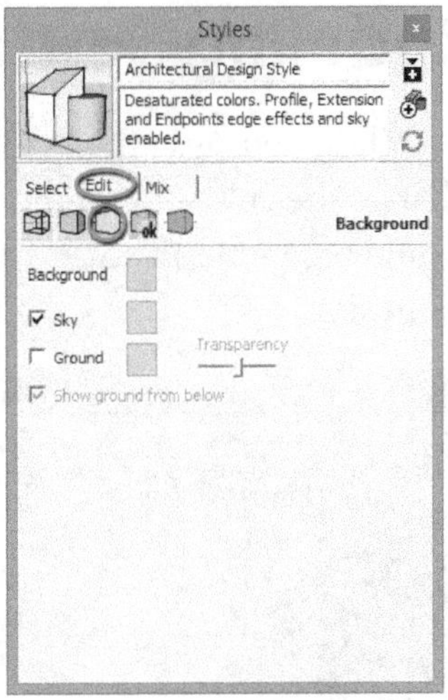

Figure 2-45
Background settings in the **Styles window**.

Watermark Settings

Watermarks are really interesting, and they allow you to create some really creative looking styles.
Watermarks let you place images on top or behind a model and blend them in with the model to create a transparent mask. (**Figure 2-46**)

Figure 2-46
Watermark settings in the **Styles window**.

TIP In a later chapter, we'll go over how you can use

watermarks to create scaling hatch materials for your models.

Modeling Settings

These settings affect various parts of your model. You can change the colors of all the various selection indicators, although I would recommend sticking with the default colors to avoid confusion.

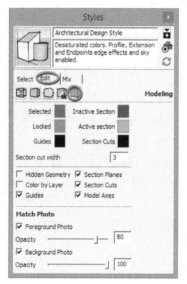

You can also view or hide Hidden Geometry, Section Planes, Color by Layer, Section Cuts, Guides, and Model Axes. (**Figure 2-47**)

TIP In most scenes created for LayOut viewports, you'll want to have Section **Planes** hidden, but Section **Cuts** active. This will allow you to show section cuts, but the actual section plane object will be hidden from the viewport.

It may also be helpful to save the style with guides disabled. In most of the viewports you create, you won't want construction guides from SketchUp to show up in LayOut.

LayOut will never show your SketchUp modeling axes in a viewport, so you don't have to worry about disabling it in the scene for a viewport. I would only disable it if I was creating an animation in SketchUp and didn't want to see the axes in it.

The match photo settings change the opacity of the photo when using the Photo Match feature in SketchUp. This feature in SketchUp allows you to place an image in your model and adapt your model position and perspective to match that in the photo.

TIP If you'd like to learn more about the **Photo Match tool**, check out my tutorial on how to model anything in the Ikea catalog at www.MasterSketchup.com/how-to-model-any-ikea-furniture-in-SketchUp/

Mix

The mix tab in the **Styles window** lets you grab settings from other styles in your library and apply them to your current style. This is a quick way to mix and match settings between styles.

You just click on a style to sample, then you click on the setting you want to apply and it will paste it into your current style.

Save Custom Styles in Model

Once you've customized a style to the way that you like it, click the "Create New Style" button in the **Styles window. (Figure 2-48)** This will save the new style to the "In Model" collection in the drop down menu.

Figure 2-48
Click the "Create New Style" button to save the style in your model.

TIP Throughout the course of modeling, you may have created a number of different styles that you don't intend on actually using. To purge unused styles, select the "In Model" collection, click the fly-out menu, and select "Purge Unused".

Save Custom Styles on Computer

As you continue to model, you'll grow tired of having to customize the styles in each new model you create. You'll want to save the custom styles that way you can use them in all of your models.

Each style is actually saved as its own file in the SketchUp folder on your computer. The default styles are saved in the folder where SketchUp is installed on your computer, but you can save custom styles in any folder on your computer.

Figure 2-49
Click and drag styles to folders to save them to your computer.

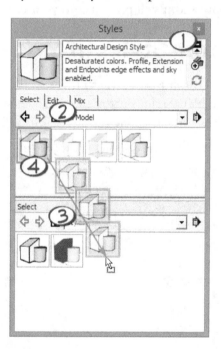

To save styles to your computer, follow these steps: Go to **Window -> Styles** to open the **Styles window**. (**Figure 2-49**)

1. Click the expand button to show the **Secondary Selection panel**.

2. In the first selection panel, select the **In Model** collection from the drop down menu.

3. In the **Secondary Selection panel**, select the collection you wish to save the custom style in.

4. Drag the **Style** thumbnail from the **In Model Selection panel** to the **Secondary Selection panel**.

Instead of adding custom styles to the default collections, it is sometimes better to create new collections and add your custom styles to those.

A collection is simply a file location on your computer that SketchUp will remember in the drop down menu. You can save style files in that folder and they will appear in the drop down menu in the **Styles window**.

To add a collection to the default collections, just use a file explorer to navigate to the SketchUp installation folder on your computer. It should be located at:

```
C:/Program Files/SketchUp/SketchUp 2015/
Styles
```

Create a new folder in this location and it will show up in the **Styles window** drop down menu.

If you want to identify a different file location for SketchUp to look for styles, you must define a folder as a new collection inside SketchUp.

To define a custom style collection, follow these steps:

1. In SketchUp, go to **Window -> Styles** to show the **Styles window**.

2. Open the fly-out window and click "Open or Create a Collection."

3. Browse to the folder location where you'd like to save your styles or create a new folder with the **Make New Folder** button.

You'll now see your new collection in the drop down menu whenever you open a new model in SketchUp. Just drag styles you create into that folder and they will be saved for future use.

Chapter Summary

✓ Styles are what change the visual style of a SketchUp model. They do not affect the structure of your model in any way.

✓ Styles are applied to the entire model.

✓ Styles can be customized using the edge, face, background, watermark, and modeling settings in the **Window -> Styles -> Edit**.

✓ Style properties can be sampled from each other using the mix tab in the **Styles window**.

✓ You can save custom styles specific to a model, or you can save them as a library item for use in any SketchUp model.

BIM modeling

With the launch of SketchUp Pro 2015, SketchUp and LayOut have really come into focus as a powerful BIM software package. Although "BIM", which stands for **Building Information Modeling,** has numerous definitions depending upon who you talk to, I like to define it as follows:

> **BIM - 3D modeling that not only captures a physical representation of an object, but includes any additional information about that object and its sub-assemblies that will aid in the design, construction, or use of the object.**

BIM is most commonly discussed in the context of architecture, but it could really apply to anything. Just think of it as data in your model in addition to the visual representation of the object.

There are a few ways SketchUp and LayOut are implementing BIM.

✓ **Dynamic Component Attributes** - By assigning attributes and values to components in SketchUp, you are attaching additional data to your model. This data can then be retrieved from inside LayOut in the form of an auto-text label.

✓ **Classifications** - SketchUp has the ability to use a predefined schema (IFC2x3 by default) to assign object types to components, and set values for object attributes. This data can then be retrieved from inside LayOut in the form of an auto-text label.

✓ **Label Tool** - In LayOut, you can read and display information about your model using the Label tool. Things like dynamic components, classifications, and measurements can all be displayed dynamically from inside LayOut.

✓ **IFC Import/Export** - One of the most important aspects of BIM is not just being able to attach data to your models, but being able to share that information universally with other software in your workflow. The IFC Import/Export feature allows you to exchange models between various software without losing any data.

Dynamic Component Attributes

The Label tool in LayOut lets you select a group or component name to be displayed as auto-text. But if you need to have additional custom text attached to components in your model, dynamic component attributes are a great way to add that information. Some examples of additional information you might want to add are:

✓ Model number/Part number

✓ Manufacturer

✓ Description

✓ Finish

✓ Specification section

You can add any custom attribute you'd like using Dynamic Components. For this example, let's add a custom attribute to a door component to identify its model number.

 **To create a custom dynamic component attribute, follow these steps:**

1. In SketchUp, select the component that you'd like to add an attribute to. (It must be a component, not a group.)

2. Go to **Window -> Component Attributes** to open the Component Attributes window.

3. Click "Add attribute".

4. Instead of selecting one of the predefined attributes from the pop up menu, type in your own, custom attribute named "ModelNumber". (**Figure 2-50**) (You cannot have any spaces in attribute names)

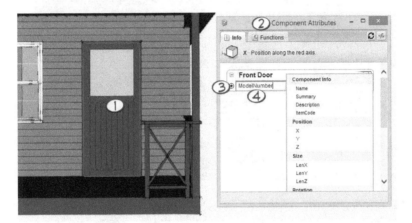

Figure 2-50
Select a component, add a custom attribute in the Component Attributes window.

5. In the text box next to the attribute, type in the model number of the component. (ACME Door D-3500) (**Figure 2-51**)

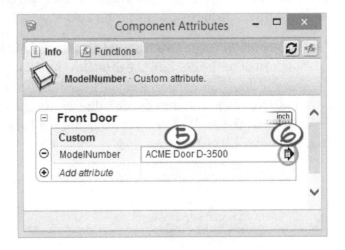

Figure 2-51
Type in a value for the attribute, then click on the details icon to set the visibility.

6. In order to make this attribute available to LayOut, we need to make it visible. Click on the Details button 🖹, and change the display rule to "Users can see this attribute". (**Figure 2-52**)

7. Click Apply.

Figure 2-52 Set
Display Rule, click
apply.

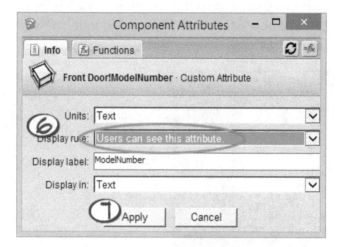

8. To verify this attribute, go to **Window -> Component Options**, and you should see the attribute in the window.

Once you've attached dynamic component attributes to your model and made them visible, you'll be able to anchor labels to the model and read those attributes from within LayOut.

In LayOut, create a viewport of the model. Use the **Label tool** to anchor a label to the door. In the drop down menu, make sure you select the door component, and you'll see the custom attribute "ModelNumber" and the custom value we attached to it in SketchUp (**Figure 2-53**). We'll learn more about the Label tool in the section "Smart Labels" on page 153.

master**Sketchup**.com

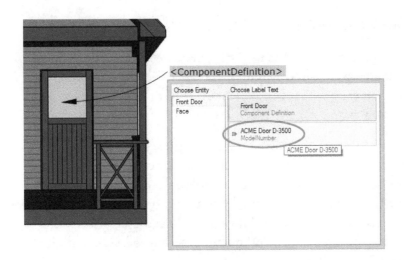

Figure 2-53
Applied label
to the door in
LayOut. Custom
attribute
available for
selection.

With advanced knowledge of dynamic components, you can create attributes that make complicated calculations and format the results in a way that you can display them in a label.

If you'd like to learn more about dynamic components, I'd suggest following some of the SketchUp self-paced tutorials at http://mastersketchup.com/dc.

Classifications

The ability to add classification tags to components in your model was introduced in SketchUp 2014. But it wasn't until 2015 where we started to see a clear purpose for tagging data to your models.

Similarly to how we created a custom dynamic component attribute, **classifications** provide the structure to add custom data to components in your model too. However, instead of defining attributes for components individually, attributes are assigned using a predefined structure, **called a schema.** The classification schema defines **object types** and **sets of attributes** that you can assign to components in your model. Once we add this data to our model, we can read it from LayOut using the **Label tool,** or export it to other software using the IFC Export. (More on IFC later)

Each object type has its own, unique set of attributes. So the attributes available to a component will depend upon which object type you classify that component as. A "roof" object type would probably have different attributes than a "window" object type.

For instance, lets say you were using a schema designed to help you tag architectural models. It might contain object types for doors, walls, windows, beams, columns, etc. You would then classify a window in your model as a "Window" object. Each object type has its own set of attributes that you can then set for each classified component. A "Window" object type might include the following attributes:

✓ Description

✓ Glass type

✓ Height

✓ Width

From the Component Options window, you can type in values for each attribute.

Classification schemas must be created ahead of time, and written in a format called XML. While SketchUp allows you to create your own classification schemas, it is very complicated, and not for the average user! You practically need to be a programmer in order to understand and format your own custom classification schema.

Fortunately, SketchUp has included an industry standard classification schema called **IFC2x3**. The IFC2x3 schema contains a structure to tag typical building object types, such as doors, walls, windows, beams, columns, etc. Once you assign a classification type to a component, you'll then be able to assign attribute values to it.

To classify an object using the IFC2x3 schema, follow these steps (Figure 2-54):

Step by Step

1. In SketchUp, go to **Window -> Entity Info** to open the Entity Info window.

2. Select a component in your model with the **Select tool**.

3. In the **Entity Info** window, click the Type drop-down menu. Click on IFC 2x3: <undefined> to expand the object type list.

4. Select **IfcWindow**.

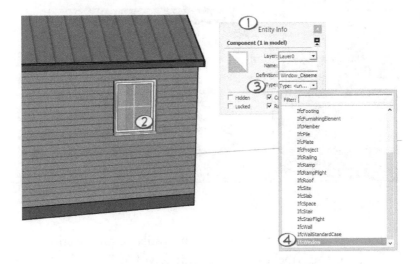

Figure 2-54
Assigning a classification object type from the Entity Info window.

The component has now been tagged as a specific object type, but all of the attributes are empty for the component. Let's add some values to the attributes.

To assign attributes to classified components, follow these steps (Figure 2-55):

Step by Step

1. In SketchUp, go to **Window -> Component Options.**

2. Select the component you'd like to assign attributes to.

3. In the **Component Options** window, scroll down until you see a black titlebar named **IFC 2x3: ifcWindow.** Click on

"Description" to expand the attribute text box.

4. In the ifcText textbox, enter "ACME Window W-3500"

5. Click Apply.

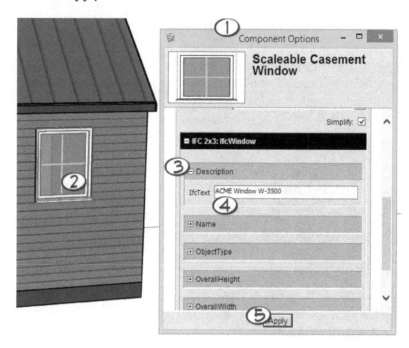

Figure 2-55
Assigning
attributes to
a classified
component.

These classification tags will now be available for selection and display using the Label tool from inside LayOut.

IFC Import/Export

Using the IFC2x3 schema classification structure, SketchUp can now also import/export the IFC filetype. IFC is a very common 3D model filetype among building industry design software, and when combined with the SketchUp Classification tool, it provides a structure for reading/writing data attached to your model (**Figure 2-56**). The file not only contains model geometry data, but it includes classification metadata for objects in your model, making it a great platform for BIM modeling.

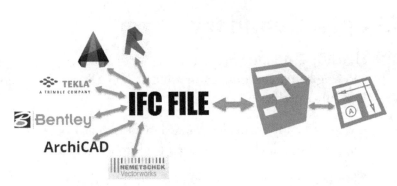

Figure 2-56
The IFC file format provides a standard file format among multiple software platforms.

IFC import/export is one of those features that if you don't know what IFC is, you probably don't need the feature, but if you do know what IFC is, then you're really excited that you now have it.

Again, if you use other software in your workflow that can interpret IFC format, this is a very useful feature because you can now take your project back and forth between different software without losing any data.

If you don't use the IFC filetype in your current workflow, then you might find the IFC2x3 classification schema to be more complicated than it needs to be for your personal needs. Unfortunately there aren't any other classification schemas available right now since this is such a new feature.

You might find it easier to use **dynamic component attributes** to add additional text data to your components, instead of using the **Classifier tool**. But in the future, you might see simplified classification schemas that you'll find helpful in your workflow.

Chapter Summary

✓ SketchUp 2015 introduced a strong set of BIM features, allowing better communication of data between SketchUp and LayOut, as well as other software.

✓ Dynamic Components let you assign custom attributes to components, which you can then read from inside LayOut.

✓ Classifications follow a predefined schema and allow you to assign object types and set attributes. The IFC2x3 schema is included in SketchUp, but you can import other schemas into SketchUp as well.

✓ SketchUp can import/export IFC files in order to incorporate other software into your workflow.

With an understanding of how to create SketchUp scenes for LayOut viewports, we'll now dive into LayOut. You'll become familiar with the LayOut interface and all the basic tools. We'll then jump into how to create a new document and start inserting viewports linked to your SketchUp model.

Once all of your viewports are set up, we'll go over all the various annotation and dimension tools provided in LayOut.

User Interface

In this section, we'll go over the LayOut user interface so you can become familiar with the program. At the end of this chapter, you will be able to navigate LayOut's menus and windows to find any tool you need.

If you'd prefer to jump right in, feel free to skip this chapter and start creating your LayOut document in the next part of this book.

The Toolbar

The toolbar is where you'll find quick access buttons to activate your most commonly used tools and functions.

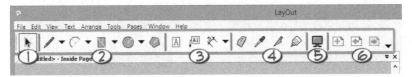

Figure 3-1
LayOut main toolbar.

1. **Select tool** – (Spacebar) This is the tool you use to select elements in paper space. You can also manipulate points and controls with the **Select tool**.

2. **Drawing tools** - This collection of tools allow you to draw lines and shapes in LayOut. Although most of your drawing will be completed in SketchUp, you will still use shapes in LayOut to create clipping masks, symbols, titleblock elements, pattern filled shapes and more.

3. **Annotation tools** - Once you insert a model into LayOut, you'll want to add dimensions, notes, and callouts. These tools will allow you to do that.

4. **Modification tools** - This collection of tools has various functions. The **Eraser tool** obviously deletes elements. The **Eyedropper tool** takes a sample of an element and then allows you to apply the style properties of that element to another. The **Slice tool** splits lines, and the **Join tool** connects overlapping lines.

5. **Presentation mode** - Clicking this button brings you into full screen presentation mode. In presentation mode, the user interface disappears and your document fills the screen. You can flip pages with a click of the mouse, and even add notes during the presentation.

6. **Navigation tools** - A few quick links to flip pages, as well as add a new page to the end of your document.

7. **Add/Remove buttons** - This drop-down menu allows you to add or remove buttons from the toolbar.

Tray Panels

The default tray panel consists of the following panels: **Shape properties, SketchUp Model properties, Annotation properties, Organization, Scrapbooks,** and **Instructor**. We'll go over each of these panels in detail in later chapters. For now, we'll do a brief overview of each one to get you acquainted to each panel.

Colors

This window will pop open automatically whenever you need to select a color for a shape fill or stroke style. Changing text color will also activate this **Colors window**.

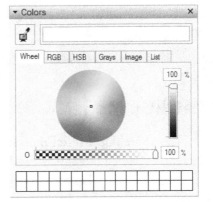

Figure 3-2
Colors panel

Shape Style

The **Shape Style window** is the main way you change the look of shapes in LayOut. The three main buttons in this panel toggle whether the shape has a fill, pattern, or stroke. You also have extensive control over whether a line is dashed, dotted, or solid, as well as how the beginning and ends of lines look. You can select a pre-existing shape, then change its properties. Or, you can activate a tool, configure it how you want it to draw from this panel, then draw the shape.

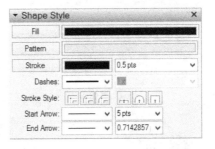

Figure 3-3
Shape Style panel.

Pattern Fill

To apply a pattern to an element, you can toggle the pattern button in the **Shape Style panel** while the element is selected, or you can drag and drop a pattern directly from this panel onto a shape.

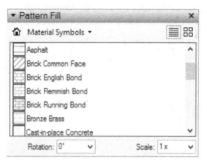

Figure 3-4
Pattern Fill panel

Alternatively, you can select an element, then click on a pattern in this panel to apply it to the selected element(s).

SketchUp Model

The **SketchUp Model panel** shows you the properties of the currently selected SketchUp model. In order to use this panel, you must have a SketchUp model viewport inserted onto one of your pages. Go to **File –> Insert** to insert a SketchUp model.

Figure 3-5
SketchUp Model panel

While I recommend creating scenes in SketchUp to assign to your viewports, you actually have a lot of control in LayOut to apply different views to your viewports.

The most important thing in this panel is the Current Scale. When your model is in Ortho mode, you can define the scale of your model so that it prints out to scale on paper.

Dimension Style

When you add dimensions to your model, the tool is very automated. You do, however, have the ability to customize your dimensions using the options in this panel. The auto scale feature usually

Figure 3-6 Dimension Style panel

works great, but if you need to define the scale of your dimensions manually, you can do that too.

Don't forget, dimensions are actually made up of lines and text, which means you need to use the **Shape Style & Text panels** in order to change the way dimensions look. The **Dimension panel** only changes properties that are specific to dimensions.

Text Style

Any type of text that is inserted into LayOut can be configured and styled from this panel. You'll find traditional text editing properties, as well as some list functions on another tab.

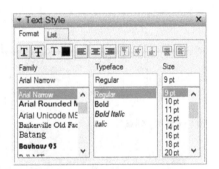

Figure 3-7 Text Style panel

(On a Mac, there is no Text Style panel. Instead, you have a Font panel.)

Pages

Figure 3-8
Pages panel

The **Pages panel** is where you manage all the pages in your LayOut document. From this panel you can add/duplicate/delete pages, as well as toggle whether or not they show up in presentation mode.

Layers

Figure 3-9
Layers panel

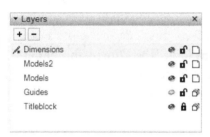

The **Layers panel** is where you manage your LayOut layers. Each page will have its own layer visibility settings, so you could have one layer visible on some pages, but not on others. You can also lock layers so any elements on them cannot be selected, destroyed or altered. Layers can also be defined as being shared across all pages or not.

Scrapbooks

Figure 3-10
Scrapbooks
panel

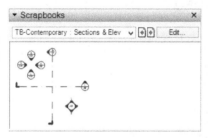

When creating drawings, a lot of times you use the same symbols and call-outs over and over throughout your projects. The scrapbook provides a way for you to use template elements in all of your projects, so you don't have to create them from scratch each time.

It also lets you use the **Eyedropper tool** to sample styles from items in your scrapbook library in order to quickly apply many style parameters to an element in a few clicks.

Instructor

When you're just starting out with LayOut, you might find it hard to remember how to use each tool. The **Instructor panel** provides a little assistance by sharing information with you about the currently selected tool. **(Figure 3-11)**

Figure 3-11
Instructor panel

Document Area

This is your working area, where you'll actually be working on your document. When you have a document open, you'll see the name of the file on a tab at the top of the document area. (**Figure 3-12**)

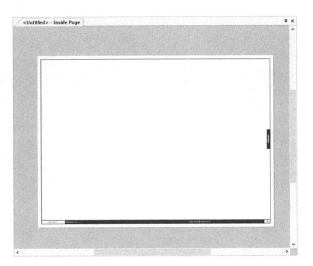

Figure 3-12
LayOut main
Document Area

Unlike SketchUp, you can have multiple files opened in LayOut at the same time. Navigating in the document area is made easy by scrolling your mouse wheel to zoom. To view a different page, select the page from the **Pages panel**.

There's also a status bar underneath the document window that will give you information about the tools you are currently using.

Chapter Summary

✓ LayOut is organized into various panels and toolbars.

✓ If you need to change a shape's fill, pattern, or stroke, use the **Style panel**. The **Color** and **Pattern panels** will pop up automatically.

✓ Each page in LayOut has its own layer visibility settings.

✓ Use the **Instructor panel** to learn more about each tool in LayOut.

LayOut Elements

Everything that is placed on a page in LayOut is considered a LayOut "element". Here are some examples of different types of elements: **(Figure 3-13)**

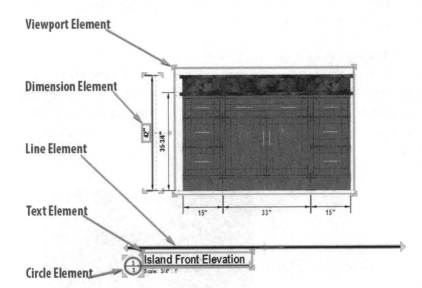

Figure 3-13
Types of LayOut elements

Viewport Element

Dimension Element

Line Element

Text Element

Circle Element

Island Front Elevation
Scale: 3/4" : 1'

Moving Elements

Unlike SketchUp, you don't need to activate any special move tool, you just click and drag elements directly using the **Select tool (Spacebar)**.

To move elements in LayOut, activate the Select tool (Spacebar) and follow these steps:

1. Click to select the element you want to move.

2. Hover over the element until your cursor changes to the move icon. Click and drag the element to move it.

You can select multiple elements at once by holding the **SHIFT** key down as you click on all the elements you'd like to select. To move the selected elements, just hover over one of the selected elements until you see the cursor change to the move icon, then click and drag.

TIP: You can also make small movements by using the arrow keys while an element is selected.

You may find it helpful to turn on the grid in order to align elements on your page. (**Figure 3-14**) To turn on the grid, go to **View -> Show Grid**. You can change the grid properties by going to **File -> Document Setup -> Grid**. You can change things such as grid color, spacing, subdivisions, whether or not to print the grid, and more.

Figure 3-14 The grid can help you align elements.

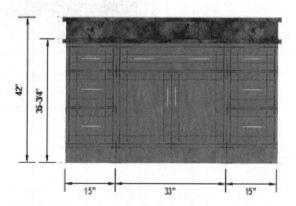

Rotating Elements

When you select an element, or multiple elements, you'll see a grip appear at the center of the selection. The position of the center grip sets the center point for rotating the element.

To rotate a selection of elements, activate the Select tool (Spacebar), and follow these steps: (Figure 3-15)

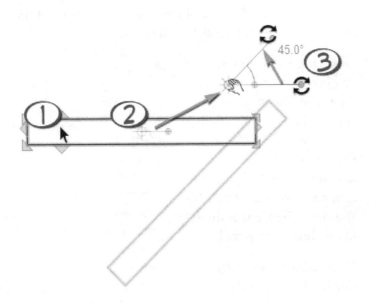

Figure 3-15 You can move the rotation point when rotating an element.

1. Select the element(s) you'd like to rotate.

2. Click and drag the center grip to the point where you'd like to rotate around.

3. Click and drag the rotation arm to rotate the element(s).

Step by Step

The center grip will always reset its position when you deselect an element, but the rotation angle will always remember the origin angle so you can reset it back to the original orientation if you decide to.

Scaling Elements

When you select an element, you'll see a blue outline around it with scaling grips at each corner and along each edge. (**Figure 3-16**) Clicking and dragging these arrowheads will allow you to scale the element.

Scaling grips

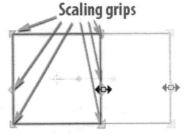

Figure 3-16 Scaling grips allow you to scale an element.

Depending upon the type of element, the contents of the element will change differently when you scale it.

✓ **Text Boxes** - Scaling a text box element will cause the text inside of it to automatically wrap within the borders of the element. **(Figure 3-17)** The font size does not change when you scale the size of the element. You must change that directly in the **Text Style panel.**

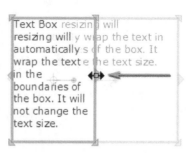

Figure 3-17 Text box scaling will reflow text within the boundaries you define.

✓ **Dimensions** - Although you can scale a dimension, it's not usually the best solution. Scaling will move all the end points of the dimension element proportionally. Usually, you don't want to affect all the end points in the dimension in the same scale, each one has a different position they need to be at. For that reason, it's always best to edit a dimension directly by double-clicking on it and manipulating its anchor points individually, instead of scaling the dimension element as a whole. **(Figure 3-18)**

Figure 3-18 Double-click dimensions to move points manually, instead of scaling them.

Double click dimensions to move points manually

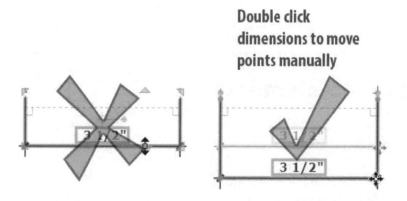

✓ **Viewports** - Resizing a viewport will change the boundary of the viewable SketchUp model. The scale of the model will also change in proportion to the viewport unless the **"Preserve Scale on Resize"** is checked in the **SketchUp Model panel**. (**Figure 3-19**)

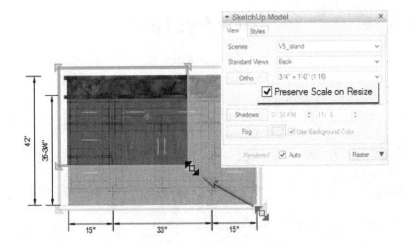

Figure 3-19
Checking "Preserve Scale on Resize" will maintain the scale of the model when scaling the boundary of the viewport.

✓ **Shapes** - When you scale a shape element, the end points inside of it will scale in proportion to the element. If you want to reposition end points manually, you can double-click on the shape and click and drag the endpoints individually. (**Figure 3-20**)

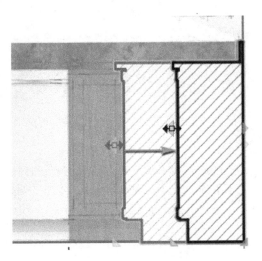

Figure 3-20
Scaling shapes will scale all the points within the shape.

✓ **Groups/Multiple Selections** - Grouped elements will scale all
of their contents equally. The same happens when you select
multiple elements and scale them.

LayOut Inference System

To help with placement of elements, LayOut can reference
different points within the page by snapping to them. There are
two types of snapping that are available in LayOut. Both can be
turned on or off. They are "Object
snap" and "Grid Snap". To enable/
disable them, go to **Arrange ->
Object snap**, and **Arrange -> Grid
Snap**.

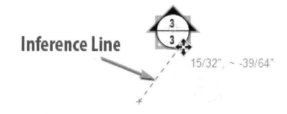

Object snap will try to lock on
to different end points on your page. Sometimes LayOut is a little
"over confident" in its inference and may try to lock on to arbitrary
points in your model. When this happens, holding the **SHIFT** key
while moving an element will lock you in to a vertical or horizontal
movement. (**Figure 3-21**)

Figure 3-21
LayOut has an
inference system
that will help you
align elements.

Inference Line

15/32", ~ -39/64"

Center Grip

The center grip that appears every time you make a selection
is not only the rotation point, but it is a movable reference point.
You can reposition it to provide a custom snapping point for an
element.

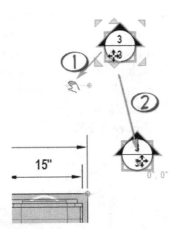

Figure 3-22 The center grip can be repositioned to create a custom snap point.

After selecting an element, click and drag the center grip to another place on the page. Now, move the element. Notice how all the inferencing is now done from the center grip (**Figure 3-22**) , and not from any of the points within the element.

Editing Elements

Elements are edited differently depending upon what type of element it is. LayOut has special panels located in the tray for each type of element.

✓ **Text Elements** - Double-click on a text element to add or edit text. Text font, size, color, etc. can be edited with the **Text Style panel**. To add a border, fill, or pattern to a text element, use the **Shape Style panel**. (**Figure 3-23**)

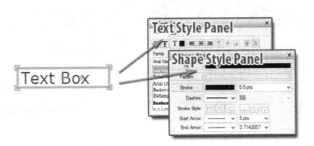

Figure 3-23 Edit text using the **Text Style** and **Shape Style** panels.

✓ **Dimension Elements** - Double-click on a dimension element to manipulate the anchor points of the dimension. To change the dimension scale, unit, and positioning, use the **Dimension Style panel**. To add a background behind the dimension text, change the end point styles, line weight, style, or color, use the **Shape Style panel**. To edit the text style of the dimension, use the **Text Style panel**. (**Figure 3-24**)

Figure 3-24
Edit dimensions
using the **Text
Style, Shape
Style**, and
**Dimension
Style** panels.

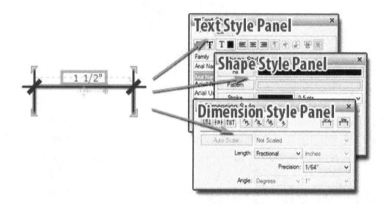

✓ **Viewport Elements** - Double-click on a viewport to enter "Model space" and manipulate the camera perspective of the model. To change the contents of a viewport, use the **SketchUp Model panel**. To add a border or background fill to a viewport use the **Shape Style panel**. (**Figure 3-25**)

Figure 3-25 Edit
viewports using
the SketchUp
model and
Shape Style
panels.

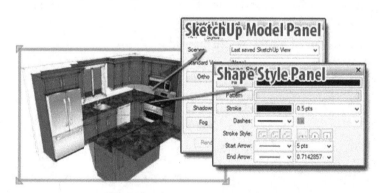

masterSketchup.com

✓ **Shape Elements** - Rectangle shapes are manipulated directly by the shape element boundary. Other shapes such as lines, circles, and polygons can be manipulated manually by double-clicking on the element and dragging the endpoints. Edit the shape's stroke, fill, pattern, and style from the **Shape Style panel**. **(Figure 3-26)**

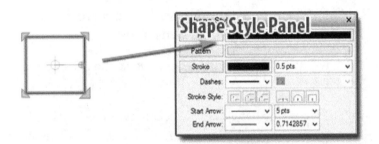

Figure 3-26 Edit shapes using the **Shape Style panel**.

✓ **Group Elements** - When you make changes to a group or a selection of elements, all of the elements within it will be affected by those changes. If you only want to edit a single element within a group, double-click on the group to open it, then select the element you want to edit.

TIP To group elements together, first select them all with the **Select tool (Spacebar)**. Next, right-click and select "Make Group". When you group elements together, they will all be moved to the same layer.

Chapter Summary

✓ Move elements using the **Select tool (Spacebar)**.

✓ Rotate elements using the arm on the center grip.

✓ You can change the location of the center grip by dragging it.

✓ LayOut elements act differently when you resize them, depending upon what type of element they are.

✓ The LayOut Inference system can be locked out using the **SHIFT** key.

✓ The different tray panels affect specific types of LayOut elements. Some panels affect more than one type of element.

Opening a New File

When you start LayOut, you'll need to open an existing document or create a new one in order to start. Rather than starting with a completely empty page, LayOut gives you the option of creating a new document based off of a template.

Templates define your paper size, default tool styles, and some of them include titleblocks. Titleblocks are frames for your pages that include things like company, project, architect, and client information.

Create a New File From a Template

Let's create a new file using the Simple Serif -> Letter Landscape template. **To create a new LayOut file using a template, follow these steps: (Figure 3-27)** To view the **Getting Started window**, go to **File -> New from Template.**

1. Select the Simple Serif folder located in **New -> Default Templates -> Titleblock -> Simple Serif.**

2. Select the Letter Landscape template.

3. Click Open.

Step by Step

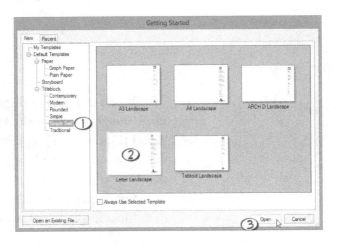

Figure 3-27
Create a new document from a template using the **Getting Started window**.

Once you open the template, you'll see a new page is created with a titleblock. Each page in LayOut represents a real page that will be printed out later on. You can create as many pages as you want in your project file.

Pages

The template we opened includes two pages to start you off: a cover page and an inside page. (**Figure 3-28**) You can view the pages in your document by clicking the expand arrow to open up the **Pages panel** on the Default Tray.

Figure 3-28 The template comes with a cover page and an inside page.

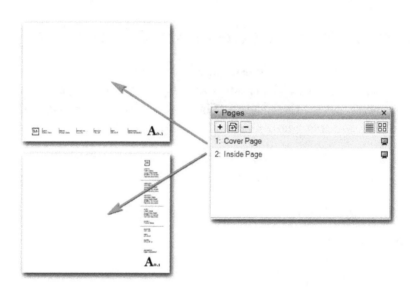

Add a Page

Figure 3-29 Click the plus sign in the **Pages panel** to add a page. Click and drag to rearrange.

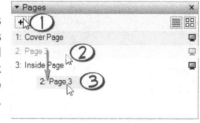

To add additional pages, click the plus sign in the Pages panel (Figure 3-29). A new page will be inserted directly after the page you are currently on. To rearrange pages, just click and drag them in the **Pages panel.**

Rename Pages

In LayOut 2013, pages are automatically numbered in the **Pages panel** depending upon their order. To rename a page to something more descriptive, double-click on the name of the page in the **Pages panel** and type in the new name.

Duplicate a Page

Another way to add a new page is to make a duplicate of an existing inside page. This will copy the page and everything inside of it. **To duplicate a page, follow these steps: (Figure 3-30)**

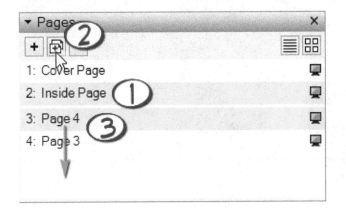

Figure 3-30
Duplicate an existing page.

1. Select the page you'd like to duplicate.

2. Click the Duplicate button.

3. Click and drag the new page to the desired order if needed.

Step by Step

Layers

Layers are an important organizational tool in LayOut. (**Figure 3-31**) They allow you to organize elements in your document in numerous ways:

✓ Organize the order in which elements appear by controlling how they overlap each other on the page.

✓ Lock layers to prevent elements from being selected or unintentionally edited.

✓ Control which elements appear on each page in your document.

✓ Create "shared layers" that can have the same elements appear on multiple pages. For example: titleblock elements.

Figure 3-31
Layers organize your model and determine the order in which elements will appear.

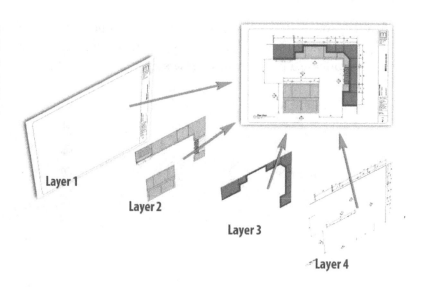

Layer 1

Layer 2

Layer 3

Layer 4

The Simple Serif template has four layers in it; **Default, Unique Elements, Cover Page,** and **On Every Inside Page.**

The visibility of layers is controlled on a page by page basis. As you browse the different pages in your document you may notice some layers are active on some, and hidden on others. You have full control over which layers are visible on each page.

Let's look at the **Layers panel** with the "**Inside Page**" page active (**Figure 3-32**).

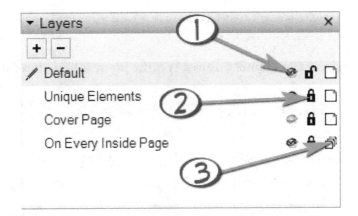

1. **Visibility** - The **Default, Unique Elements,** and **On Every Inside Page** layers are visible on this page. You can tell by the eye icon next to the layer name. You can toggle the visibility of a layer on each page by clicking this icon.

2. **Lock/Unlock** - The **Default** layer is the only unlocked layer in the document. If you lock a layer, it will be locked throughout the document. When a layer is locked, you won't be able to select or manipulate any of the elements that reside on that layer. To toggle, just click on the lock icon.

3. **Shared Layers** - The **On Every Inside Page** layer is a shared layer. Any element that is placed on this layer will show up on all of the pages in the document, unless the page has the layer hidden. This is great for repeating elements such as titleblocks or watermarks. You can toggle whether elements repeat on every page or not by clicking the page icon.

Insert an Element On a Layer

Before inserting any elements into LayOut, you should always look at the **Layers panel** and make sure you have the correct layer activated. Elements will be placed on whichever layer you have currently active.

You can identify which layer is currently active by the pencil icon next to the layer name (**Figure 3-33**). If you need to activate a different layer, simply click on the layer name in the **Layers panel**.

To insert an element onto a specific layer, follow these steps:

Figure 3-33
The pencil icon indicated the currently active layer.

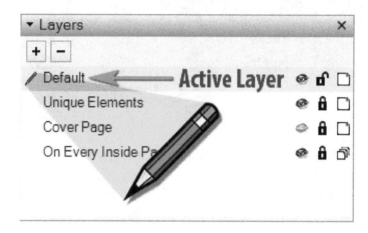

 **Step by Step**

1. Select the layer you want to insert an element onto. Verify the active layer by looking for the pencil icon next to the layer name.

2. Insert the element on the page in your document.

Re-assigning layers

You can see which layer an element is assigned to by selecting it (**Figure 3-34**). A small black square will appear next to the layer that element resides on in the **Layers panel**. Selecting an element that is not on the active layer will not change your currently active layer. The only way to change the active drawing layer is to select it in the **Layers panel**.

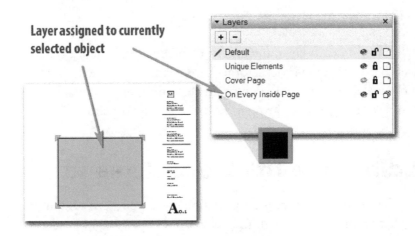

Layer assigned to currently selected object

Figure 3-34
When you select an element, you'll see the layer it's assigned to by a small black square next to the layer.

Sometimes you accidentally place an element on the wrong layer.

To assign an element to a different layer, follow these steps: (Figure 3-35)

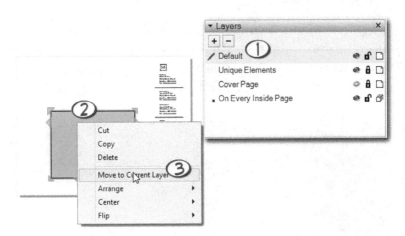

Figure 3-35
You can reassign an element to a different layer.

1. Activate the layer you want to move the element to by clicking on it in the **Layers panel**.

2. Right-click on the element.

3. Select "**Move to Current Layer**".

Step by Step

Element Order Inside Layers

Within each layer, the order in which each element overlaps each other is called the "Z order". You can change the Z-order of an element by right-clicking an element, going to arrange, and selecting either "Bring to Front", "Bring Forward", "Send Backward", or "Send to Back".

Editing the Titleblock Elements

To edit the elements on your titleblock, you need to double-click on the element with the **Select tool (Spacebar)** in order to open it. Zoom in by scrolling your mouse wheel. You need to know which layer an element is on in order to make sure the layer is not locked. If you click on an element and it doesn't do anything, it's probably on a locked layer.

Change the Logo

Let's go ahead and customize the Simple Serif template with your company info, and save it as a new template for later use. If you haven't already, open up a new "file from template" from the beginning of this chapter and **follow these steps: (Figure 3-36)**

Figure 3-36
Unlock the **Cover Page** layer and delete the default logo.

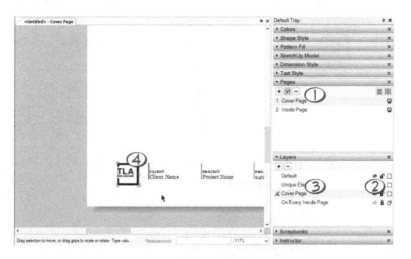

1. Go to the **Cover** page by navigating to it from the **Pages panel**.

2. Unlock the **Cover Page** layer by clicking the unlock icon on the **Layers panel**.

3. Click on the **Cover Page** layer name to make it the active drawing layer.

4. Click on the default logo to select it, and tap Delete on your keyboard to delete it.

Figure 3-37
Insert a new logo and move into position.

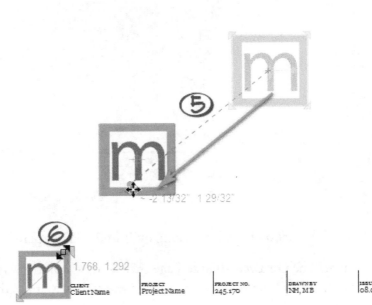

5. To insert a new logo, go to **File -> Insert** and select an image to place in your template as your logo. (If you don't have a logo, you can skip this step.) Click and drag the inserted image to move it.

6. Drag one of the blue arrows around the border of the image to

resize it.

7. Relock the **Cover Page** layer to prevent any accidental editing of the cover page elements.

Change the Text

You'll want to change the placeholder text on the titleblock as well. The cover page has project specific information, so we'll just leave the placeholder text there for now. **To edit text, follow these steps: (Figure 3-38)**

Figure 3-38 Edit company info on the Inside Pages titleblock.

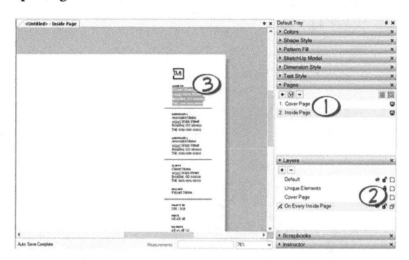

1. Go to the **Inside Page** by clicking on it in the **Pages panel**.

2. Unlock the **On Every Inside Page** shared layer from the **Layers panel**. (This layer repeats elements on every page that has this layer visible.)

3. Double-click on the company name with the **Select tool (Spacebar)** to make the text editable. Type in your company info.

4. Re-lock the "On Every Inside Page" once you finish editing.

Change the logo on this page the same way you did it for the cover page. Next, we'll save this as a template for future projects.

Go to **File -> Save As Template** to save this document as a template. Select a folder you'd like to save it in and click Ok.

Chapter Summary

✓ Templates can be used to create pre-configured titleblock pages.

✓ Navigate the pages of your document from the **Pages panel**.

✓ Elements on "shared" layers will appear on every page in your document as long as the layer is not hidden.

✓ LayOut layers differ from SketchUp layers.

Insert SketchUp Models

The most powerful feature in LayOut is the ability to create a dynamic link to your SketchUp model through the use of viewports. Viewports can remain linked to the SketchUp file they were created from. If you make changes to the SketchUp model, you can tell the viewport to update its model reference and it will show the updated model.

Step by Step

To insert a SketchUp model viewport into your LayOut document, follow these steps:

1. In LayOut, go to **File -> Insert.**

2. Navigate to the **Kitchen.skp** model included with this book, and click open.

Figure 3-39 A model viewport shows the last saved SketchUp view by default.

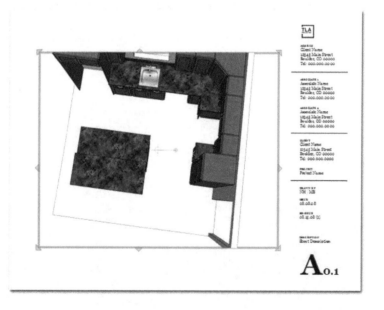

Setting the Scene

When you insert a new model viewport into LayOut, it will

show you the view of the model as you last saved it in SketchUp. (**Figure 3-39**) You're going to want to assign a specific SketchUp scene to this viewport. If you leave it set to "Last saved SketchUp View", the view will change every time you update the model. **To set the scene of a SketchUp model viewport, follow these steps: (Figure 3-40)**

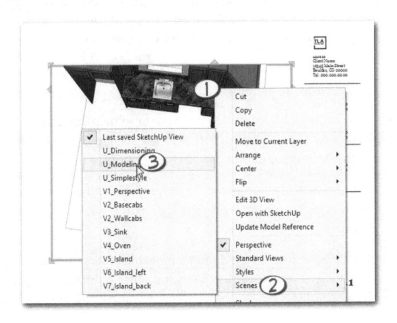

Figure 3-40
Assign a viewport to a scene.

1. Right-click on the viewport.

2. Select the scene you want from the **Scenes** fly-out menu. For this example, select the scene labeled "**V3_Sink**".

    Alternatively, you can select a scene by going to the **SketchUp Model panel** while the viewport is selected, and choose a scene there.

Step by Step

Positioning the Viewport

Once you've assigned a scene to a viewport, the next thing you'll want to do is resize and position the viewport to roughly where you want it to go on the page. Is this viewport going to take up the entire page, or is it going to be one of many viewports sharing space on the page?

When you hover over a viewport with the **Select tool (Spacebar)**, the cursor will change to a move tool and will allow you to move a viewport around on the page. Just click and drag the viewport around to position it elsewhere on the page. Here are some tips to help you with positioning your viewport.

✓ Go to **View -> Show Grid** to make a grid guide appear on the page to assist in aligning elements.

✓ LayOut has a built in Inference System to help you align elements. If you'd like to turn off Object snap or Grid Snap, go to the **Arrange menu** to toggle those options.

✓ You can make fine adjustments to the positioning of a viewport by using the arrow keys on your keyboard while an element is selected.

✓ Each element in SketchUp has a movable center grip that can be relocated to help with referencing other points on the page for positioning.

Sizing the Viewport

The **size of the viewport window** is defined separately from the **scale of the SketchUp model**. The size of the viewport window determines how much of the SketchUp model fills the page. The SketchUp model scale accurately sets the "zoom level" of the model in the viewport.

To change the size of the viewport, click and drag any of the blue triangles that appear along the edge of the viewport while it is selected.

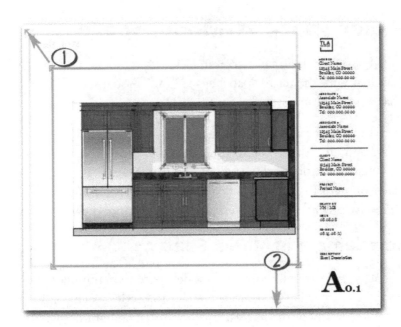

Figure 3-41
Resize viewports
by dragging the
border.

By default, the scale size of the model will change in relationship to the size of the viewport. As you increase the size of the viewport, the SketchUp model will scale larger as well. If you don't want the SketchUp model to scale when you resize the model, go to the **SketchUp Model panel -> View tab ->** check **"Preserve Scale on Resize"**.

Follow these tips when resizing viewports:

✓ Grab one of the corner arrows to scale both the height and width at the same time.

✓ Hold **SHIFT** while dragging one of the arrows to scale the viewport while maintaining the same aspect ratio.

✓ While holding any of the arrows along the edge of a viewport, you can drag your mouse out to reference any point on the page, even if it doesn't fall within the bounds of the viewport.

Paper Space vs. Model Space

For people familiar with AutoCAD type programs, you may be familiar with the terms "paper space" and "model space". LayOut has a similar functionality.

Paper space is the work area that exists in the LayOut environment. This is where you can add viewports, dimensions, annotations, title block elements, etc. Model space is an environment that exists inside of viewports. Everything in the **SketchUp Model panel** affects elements in model space.

Edit Camera in Model Space

LayOut lets you jump into model space to manipulate the camera perspective of your viewports. In model space you have access to many of the navigational tools you are familiar with from SketchUp. This is a great way to quickly scale the models inside viewports. **To enter model space and scale a model, follow these steps: (Figure 3-42)**

Figure 3-42
Double-click a viewport to enter Model Space, scroll to zoom.

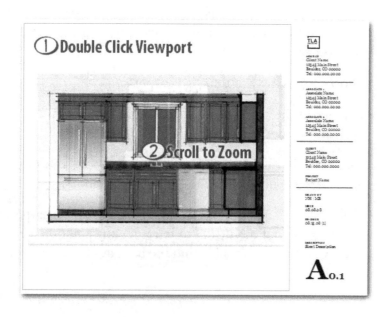

1. Double-click on a viewport with the **Select tool (Spacebar)** to enter model space.

2. Scroll with the mouse to zoom in and out. This changes the drawing scale of your model.

3. Hold down the **SHIFT** key to activate the **Pan tool**. This will allow you to reposition your model within the viewport window.

4. To quickly scale the model to fill the area of the viewport, right-click and select "Zoom Extends".

Be aware that whenever you change any of the camera settings of a model viewport, you are modifying it from scene settings you assigned to it. You will know you have modified a scene by looking at the **SketchUp Model panel** while a viewport is selected. In the scene selection box, you'll see the words "(Modified)". (**Figure 3-43)**

Whenever you update the model reference for a scene that has been modified in LayOut, it will only update the scene content with any changes you made to the SketchUp entities. It will not make any changes to the camera or style settings even if you've changed the scene settings in SketchUp.

Figure 3-43
Entering model space will make the scene "Modified".

The good news is that you don't have to worry about the scale changing back to the scene default when you update the model reference.

But, if you made changes to the scene style or camera settings in SketchUp and would like them to show up in the viewport, you'll need to select that scene again from the scenes drop down menu. Just be aware that any dimensions you may have attached to the viewport will likely need to be redone because the model scale will reset.

Ortho and Perspective Viewports

There are two main types of viewports: **Orthogonal** viewports and **perspective** viewports. (**Figure 3-44**) With an orthogonal viewport, you can define a specific scale relative to the paper you will be printing the drawings on. Perspective viewports cannot be assigned a scale, however, because the size of the elements get smaller when they are further away in the scene.

Figure 3-44
Orthogonal
mode vs.
Perspective
mode.

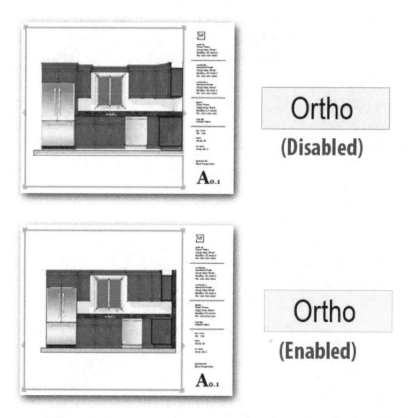

Although you can add dimensions to any type of viewport in LayOut, it is preferred to use an orthogonal viewport whenever you plan on adding dimensions. In ortho mode, dimensions are shown at the same scale, while in perspective mode dimensions are scaled depending upon where the pick points are made in the viewport.

You should save the perspective settings in the SketchUp scene before importing your model to LayOut. However, you can manually override the scene settings in the **SketchUp Model panel** by clicking the **Ortho button**.

Scaling Perspective Viewports

You can change the size and orientation of perspective viewports using the camera tools described in the previous section. Although it is best to orient your camera settings in SketchUp and save them as a scene, it is generally acceptable to orbit and zoom perspective viewports in LayOut's model space.

Scaling Orthogonal Viewports

Once you set a rough scale by zooming your viewport in model space, **follow these steps to set a standardized drawing scale: (Figure 3-45)**

Step by Step

1. Select the viewport.

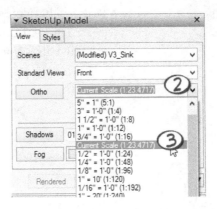

Figure 3-45
Set viewport scale from the **SketchUp Model panel**.

2. In the **SketchUp Model panel,** expand the drop down menu that shows the current scale.

3. In the list of standard scales, the current scale will show up in between the two scales it is closest to. Select the one above or below it to change the scale of the viewport.

The viewport will then change to match the drawing scale you just selected. If the size of the model looks good to you, it's a good idea to check the box "Preserve Scale on Resize" in the **SketchUp Model panel** to ensure that your viewport scale doesn't change if you decide to resize your viewport window at any point.

TIP Of course, if you know the exact drawing scale you want to set the viewport to, you can set the scale from the drop down menu immediately after importing the model instead of zooming it manually.

Raster, Vector, & Hybrid

There are three different rendering settings you can choose from for your viewport. Each one has a different affect upon the look of your viewport and the processing performance in LayOut.

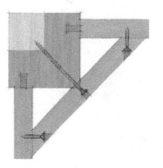

✓ **Raster** - When you set a viewport to raster, LayOut will generate an image of the scene and save that as what you see in the viewport. This will show all textures and sketchy edges from the SketchUp style. This is the fastest setting for a viewport, but you loose quality when you zoom in and the viewport can appear pixelated.

✓ **Vector** - A vector viewport will replace all sketchy edge styles and textures for solid colors, but will produce accurate, crisp edges. Edges will not pixelate when you zoom in. Clipping planes and Xray styles will not work in vector mode. This can take more processing power to generate vector viewports.

✓ **Hybrid** - Hybrid will produce vector edges, but will generate a raster image of the textures. This is also processor intensive.

To switch between raster, vector, and hybrid modes, select a viewport, then select a mode from the drop down menu in the **SketchUp Model panel**. **(Figure 3-46)**

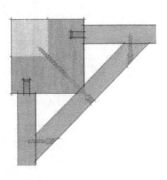

Figure 3-46
Select rendering mode from the **SketchUp Model panel**.

Controlling Line Weight

In LayOut, you have the ability to adjust the lineweight of edges in your viewport. You can only set one lineweight per viewport. If you want to have different line weights in different parts of your model, you'll have to isolate those parts onto their own viewport and overlay them. See the chapter on stacking viewports to learn how to do that.

Figure 3-47
Change line weight from the **SketchUp Model panel,** under the **Styles tab**.

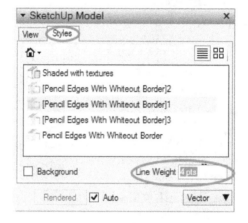

To change the lineweight of the edges in your viewport, select the viewport, then click on the **Styles tab** in the **SketchUp Model panel**. Type in a new line weight in the **Line Weight text box** in the lower right hand corner of the panel. (**Figure 3-47**)

Updating SketchUp Models

During the course of a project, it is likely that you will need to make some changes to your SketchUp model. Your viewports won't update with the changes until you tell them to, so you don't have to worry about inadvertently messing up your viewports.

To update all of the SketchUp model references in your LayOut document, follow these steps: (Figure 3-48)

Figure 3-48
Update your model reference from the Document Setup window.

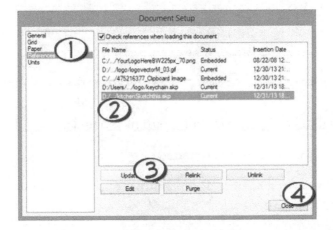

1. Go to **File -> Document Setup -> References**.

2. Select the SketchUp model file you'd like to update.

3. Click Update. Wait for the file to load, then click close.

Step by Step

Follow these steps to update your model right from the document page: (Figure 3-49)

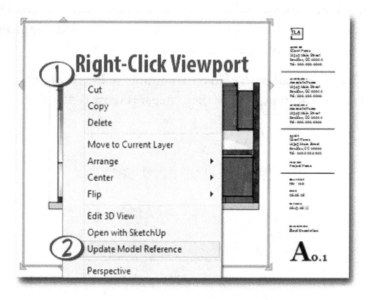

Step by Step

1. Right-click on the viewport you'd like to update.

2. Select **Update Model Reference**.

All viewports in your document that reference that same model file will now be updated.

Most of the times I'll have SketchUp and LayOut open at the same time so I can bounce back and forth, making small adjustments to my SketchUp model to get it to look just right.

One thing to remember is to make sure you save your SketchUp model after making changes before you try to update the reference in LayOut. It's easy to forget!

Clipping Masks

LayOut gives you the ability to create clipping masks, which is great for creating custom boundaries around a viewport. Instead of having a rectangular viewport shape, you can create a custom shape and link it to the viewport as a clipping mask.

To create a clipping mask, follow these steps: (Figure 3-50, Figure 3-51)

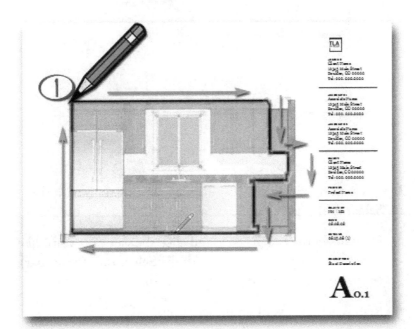

Figure 3-50 Use the **Line tool** **(L)** to draw a shape over your viewport.

1. To draw a shape over your model, activate the **Line tool (L)**. Hover over a point in your viewport until the cursor snaps to it. Click to start drawing. Continue to click different points in your viewport until you return back to your origin.

Step by Step

Figure 3-51
Create a clipping
mask from
the shape you
created.

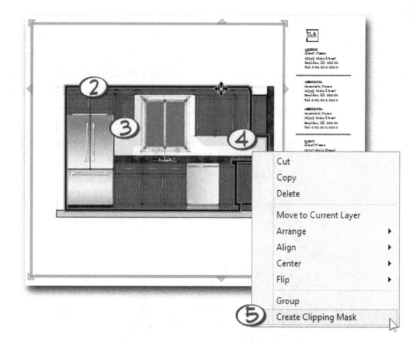

2. Click on the shape you just drew by clicking on it with the **Select tool (Spacebar)**.

3. Hold down the **SHIFT** key, and click the viewport you'd like to create a clipping mask for with the **Select tool (Spacebar)**. Make sure both the viewport and the shape are selected.

4. Right-click over your group selection.

5. Select **Create Clipping Mask**.

    The shape will then disappear but you will see the viewport contained within the boundaries of the shape. To remove a clipping mask, right-click and select **Release Clipping Mask**. If you need to edit the shape after creating a clipping mask, double-click on the viewport to enter the group, then double-click on one of the shape's edges to edit it. You can also edit the viewport in this manner.

Add a Border to Clipping Mask

Once you've created a clipping mask, you may want to add a border around the edges to define the boundaries of the shape. By creating a clipping mask between a shape and a viewport, those elements become grouped and can be edited like any other element in LayOut.

To add a border to a masked viewport, follow these steps: (Figure 3-52)

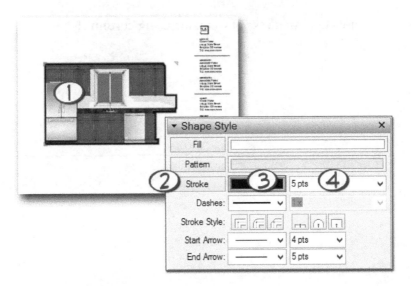

Figure 3-52 Add a border to your clipping mask

1. Select the element you'd like to add a border to.

2. In the **Shape Style panel**, click the **Stroke button**.

3. Double-click the stroke swatch to select a color for the stroke.

4. Set the size of the stroke by typing in a width in the stroke width box.

Chapter Summary

✓ Insert a SketchUp Model viewport from **File -> Insert**.

✓ Create scenes ahead of time in SketchUp, and recall them from the viewport in LayOut.

✓ The viewport size is different from the SketchUp model scale.

✓ Enter model space by double-clicking on a viewport.

✓ Orthogonal models can be assigned a fixed scale.

✓ You can update viewports globally or one at a time.

✓ Create clipping masks of elements using custom shapes.

Adding Dimensions

The **Dimension tool (D)** allows you to measure and display dimensions of models shown in viewports. The tool snaps to points in your model to create accurate dimensions, and it can automatically detect the scale of the model. (**Figure 3-53**)

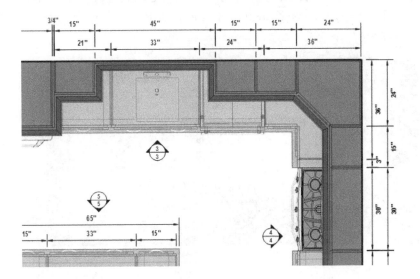

Figure 3-53
Insert accurately scaled dimensions into your LayOut document.

You have complete control over the look of your dimension lines including the line weight, style, placement, end point style, color, unit of measurement, precision, scale, text placement and font. LayOut can create linear and angular measurements.

Creating a Dimension Line

In order to create an accurate dimension line, you have to be able to pick points in a viewport that accurately represent the dimension you want to measure. This should be something to keep in mind as you organize your SketchUp model and create your scenes for LayOut viewports.

To create a linear dimension line, follow these steps: (Figure 3-54)

1. Activate the **Linear Dimension tool (D).**

2. Select the correct layer that you want dimensions to reside on. In the **Layers panel**, click on the **Dimensions** layer to activate it. (If you don't have a **Dimensions** layer, create one and position it above all other layers)

Figure 3-54
Insert linear dimensions into your LayOut document.

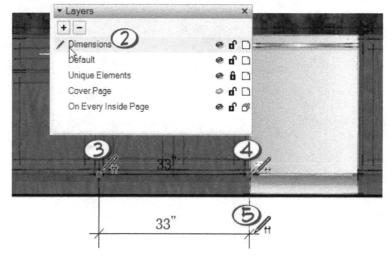

3. Snap to a point on a viewport where you'd like to measure from and click to start the dimension.

4. Snap to a second point and click to define the second measurement point.

5. Drag the mouse towards the direction you'd like the dimension line to sit, click to place.

Editing Dimensions

When you edit a dimension, you'll be referencing a number of different panels in LayOut. (**Figure 3-55**)

✓ To edit the look of the dimension lines and intersections, you'll use the **Shape Style panel**.

✓ To change the scale, precision, unit of measurement, and dimension text box alignment, you'll use the **Dimension Style panel**.

✓ To format the dimension text, you'll use the **Text Style panel**.

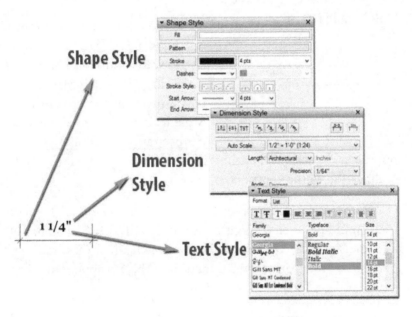

Shape Style

Dimension Style

Text Style

Figure 3-55
The various panels you will be using to edit dimensions.

Dimension Scale

When you pick two points in a model, LayOut will try to determine the scale of the viewport model and match the dimension scale to it. This is the **Auto Scale** feature built in to the dimension tool.

Figure 3-56 It's important to make sure the dimension scale matches the viewport scale.

When you insert a dimension, you need to make sure the scale of the dimension matches the scale of the viewport.

Although most of the times it guesses the scale correctly, you always want to double check to make sure. (**Figure 3-56**) I also recommend turning the **Auto Scale** feature off once a dimension has been placed because sometimes the scale will change unexpectedly if you make a small modification to the viewport.

TIP To edit the default settings of the **Dimension tool**, select the tool first, then configure the settings BEFORE creating the dimension. The **Dimension tool** will remember these settings the next time you create a dimension. This tip applies to every tool in LayOut.

To turn off Auto Scale and set the dimension scale manually, follow these steps: (Figure 3-57, Figure 3-58)

1. Select the dimension(s) you'd like to set the scale for.

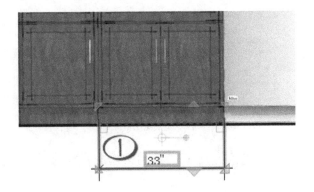

Figure 3-57
Select the dimension you want to edit.

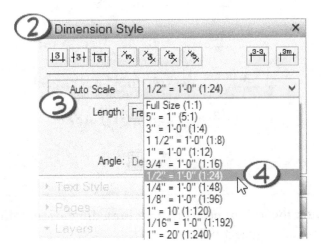

Figure 3-58
Disable auto-scale and set your own scale manually.

2. Expand the **Dimension Style panel**.

3. Click the **Auto Scale button** to disable Auto Scale.

4. Click the drop down menu and select the scale for the dimension(s).

Unit of Measurement & Precision

If the dimension is not the correct unit of measurement, you can change it in the **Dimension Style panel**. LayOut offers a number of various units of measurement along with different display styles as well. (**Figure 3-59**)

Figure 3-59
Various units of
measurement
available in
LayOut.

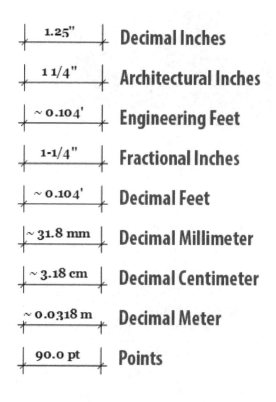

⊢ 1.25" ⊣	**Decimal Inches**
⊢ 1 1/4" ⊣	**Architectural Inches**
⊢ ~ 0.104' ⊣	**Engineering Feet**
⊢ 1-1/4" ⊣	**Fractional Inches**
⊢ ~ 0.104' ⊣	**Decimal Feet**
⊢ ~ 31.8 mm ⊣	**Decimal Millimeter**
⊢ ~ 3.18 cm ⊣	**Decimal Centimeter**
⊢ ~ 0.0318 m ⊣	**Decimal Meter**
⊢ 90.0 pt ⊣	**Points**

To set the unit of measurement for a dimension, follow these steps: (Figure 3-60)

Step by Step

1. Select the dimension you'd like to edit.

Figure 3-60
Change the unit
of measurement
of a dimension.

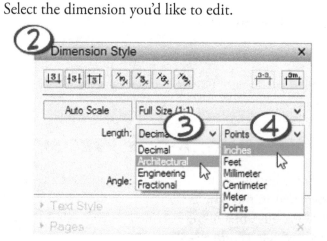

2. Expand the **Dimension Style panel.**

3. Select a dimension display type from the drop-down menu.

4. Select the unit of measurement from the drop-down menu.

You can also define the level of precision, in order to round the measurement to the nearest unit interval you define. (**Figure 3-61**)

Don't confuse accuracy with precision. LayOut will accurately snap to points in your model viewport and measure the actual dimension. The key is to make sure you are snapping to the correct points in your viewport.

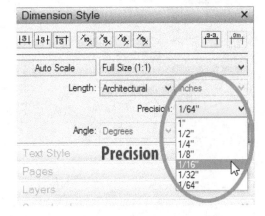

Figure 3-61
Change the precision of a dimension.

If you have multiple end points close together in your model, it will be harder to snap to the correct point when placing dimensions. In cases like this, there are a few things you can do to get around this:

✓ Zoom in further while dimensioning so you can verify you are snapping to the correct point.

✓ Save a scene in SketchUp that only saves style. Set that style to something with simple, straight lines. Switch to this scene temporarily while placing dimensions if you are having trouble seeing where end points are because of the style you are using.

✓ Decrease the precision of your dimension in order to compensate for an inaccurately snapped dimension. (I don't recommend this because you should be making sure you are snapping to the correct points in your viewport.)

Dimension Text Placement

In the **Dimension Style panel**, you can change the alignment of the dimension text in relationship with the dimension line. (

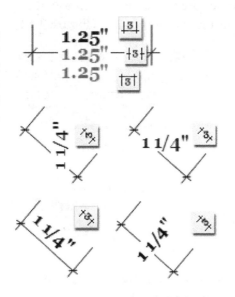

Figure 3-62) Click on the different alignment buttons at the top of the panel to align the text above, below, or in the middle of the line. You can also toggle whether the text is vertical, horizontal, aligned, or perpendicular to the dimension line.

Figure 3-62 LayOut offers a number of different dimension alignment options.

If the default text placement options are not enough to get the text exactly where you need it, you can manually relocate it as well.

To manually place the dimension text box, follow these steps: (Figure 3-63)

Step by Step

1. Double-click on a dimension to edit it.

2. Click and drag the dimension text box to wherever you'd like it to be. You can also change the text justification within the text box from the **Text Style panel.**

Figure 3-63 You can manually override the dimension text box placement.

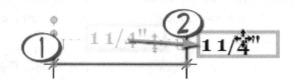

Exploding Dimensions

Sometimes, when creating small dimensions, you'll notice the dimension text background overlaps the dimension line in an undesirable manner. If you can't overcome this effect by repositioning the text, your only option is to "explode" the dimension.

When you explode a dimension element, LayOut converts it into individual LayOut entities. This means the text is not a "smart element" anymore, it is just a block of text. The lines of the dimension do not snap to the model anymore, they are just lines.

When you explode a dimension, you can write anything in the text block or delete it altogether if you want. **Only explode a dimension as a last resort, since you lose all of the benefits of a dimension line when you do that.**

Dimension Shape & Text Style

There are many different dimension shape styles to choose from in LayOut. You have control over the line weight, color, start arrow, end arrow, font, and text size.

To change the style of the dimension line, select the dimension, and open the Shape Style panel. With the dimension selected, you can change the following characteristics of the dimension line: (Figure 3-64)

1. Line stroke (thickness) and color

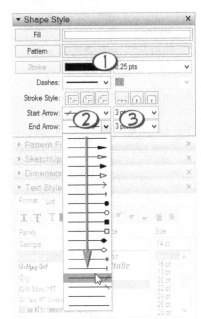

Figure 3-64
Customize dimension style using the **Shape Style panel**.

2. Start & end arrows

3. Arrow sizes

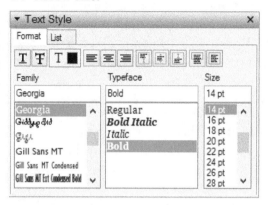

Figure 3-65 Customize the dimension text using the **Text Style panel.**

To change the style of the dimension text, expand the **Text Style panel** to change the font, size, color, style, alignment, and justification. (**Figure 3-65**)

Chapter Summary

✓ Lock dimension scale by disabling **Auto Scale** in the **Dimensions panel**.

✓ Change dimension leader style from the **Shape Style panel**.

✓ Explode dimensions for control over the entities, but only as a last resort.

✓ Change dimension settings from the **Dimension Style panel**.

✓ Change text style from the **Text Style panel.**

Advanced Dimensions

There are some additional tricks you can use for placing dimensions that will help you create them faster and easier.

Non-Parallel Dimensions

In LayOut, the two points you are trying to measure do not need to be parallel with the dimension line you want to place. Just pick the two points you want to measure, then drag your mouse towards the direction you want it to measure parallel from. (**Figure 3-66**)

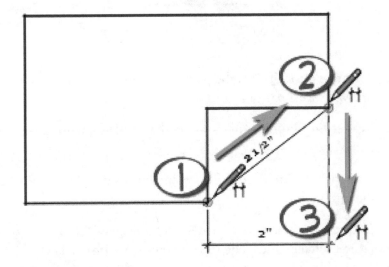

Figure 3-66
You can place dimensions even if the points are not parallel to the dimension line.

LayOut will typically snap to vertical and horizontal orientations, as well as parallel from the two points you picked.

Adjusting Dimension Leaders

Double-click on a dimension to edit it. You'll notice a bunch of blue dots at various points on the dimension. You can edit these points by clicking and dragging them. See (**Figure 3-67**) to learn what these points do.

Figure 3-67
Adjust end points by double -clicking on a dimension and dragging the end point.

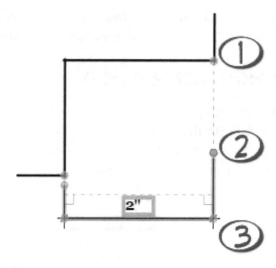

1. **Anchor Point** - This is the point from which the dimension line will measure from.

2. **Leader End Point** - This is where the visible dimension leg ends.

3. **Dimension Line Point** - This point adjusts the position of the dimension line.

    Just be aware that if you have **Auto Scale** enabled, the dimension is likely to change scale if you mess with the anchor point. Moving the anchor point will change the dimension text automatically according to the scale the dimension is set to.

Quick Dimension Offsets

When you start placing dimensions, you'll notice the LayOut inference system will help you align dimensions with each other and allow you to reference points on the page as well.

An even faster way to create consistently offset dimensions is to double-click when you select your second dimension point. LayOut remembers the offset of the last dimension you placed, so when you double-click to set a new dimension, it will automatically match the same offset as the previous one.

The dimension will appear above or below the two points you picked depending upon if you clicked from left to right, or right to left.

Angular Dimensions

You can create angular dimensions in LayOut using the **Angular Dimension tool**.

To create an angular dimension, follow these steps: (Figure 3-68) Switch the Dimension tool to angular by selecting it from the drop-down menu.

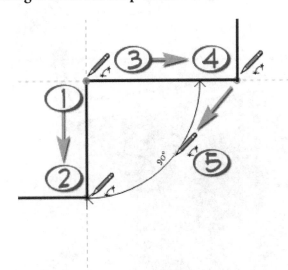

Figure 3-68
Angular dimensions can be placed in LayOut as well.

1. Click on a point that is in line with the first edge of the angle you want to dimension.

2. Click a second point to define the first edge.

3. Click a third point on the second edge you want to measure the angle to.

4. Click a fourth point to define the second edge.

5. Position your mouse on the inside of the angle to provide the acute angle measurement or on the outside to provide the obtuse measurement. Click to place the angle dimension.

Perspective Viewports

If you insert a perspective viewport into your LayOut document, you can add accurate dimensions to the model even though the model is not orthographic. (**Figure 3-69**)

Figure 3-69
Perspective viewports can be accurately dimensioned.

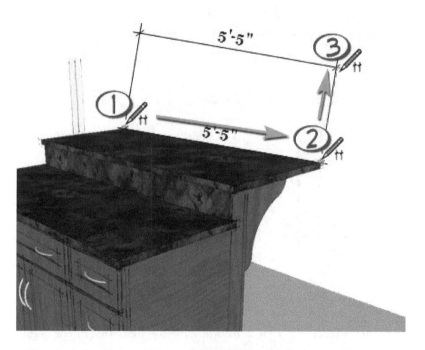

Just use the **Dimension tool (D)** to pick two points in your model and LayOut will **Auto Scale** the dimension to match the measurement from the SketchUp model.

There's no real surefire way to verify that you picked the points accurately so be careful when using this method and make sure the dimension is snapping to the correct points and reading the proper measurement.

TIP While dragging a dimension to its position, you can hold the **ALT key (Command key on Mac)** to have greater control over the positioning of the dimension line.

Chapter Summary

✓ Dimension anchor points can be manipulated by double-clicking on a dimension element.

✓ You can quickly duplicate dimension line offsets by double-clicking the end point of a dimension when placing it.

✓ You can measure acute or obtuse angles in LayOut.

✓ Perspective model viewports can be dimensioned accurately.

Annotations

In LayOut, you can also add text, or text with leaders. This is great for identifying different parts in your viewport, or adding notes and conditions.

Text Box

You'll be using the **Shape Style panel** and the **Text Style panel** to control the look of the text box.

To insert a text box, activate the layer you'd like to add the text to, activate the Text Box tool (T) and follow these steps:

1. Click and drag to define a boundary box for the text. **(Figure 3-70)**

Figure 3-70
Define a text boundary box by click and drag.

Figure 3-71 Text auto-wrapping.

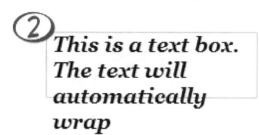

This is a text box. The text will automatically wrap

2. Type your text, press ESC to finish.**(Figure 3-71)** If your text is longer than one line, it will automatically wrap to the next

line. However, if your text is larger than the boundary box you originally created, the text will be cut off. You'll be able to tell if you have overflow text by a small red arrow at the lower right corner of the text box.

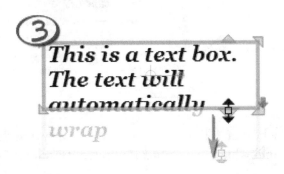

Figure 3-72
Resize overflow text boundary boxes to reveal the hidden text.

3. If you have overflow text, click and drag the lower boundary down further to give the text box more space to show the enclosed text. **(Figure 3-72)**

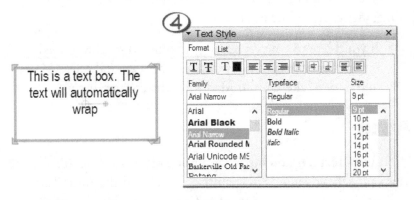

Figure 3-73 The **Text Style panel** will edit the text style.

4. To change the font, size, color, justification, or other styles, use the **Text Style panel** while the text box is selected. **(Figure 3-73)**

Figure 3-74
The **Shape Style panel** will edit the text box element style.

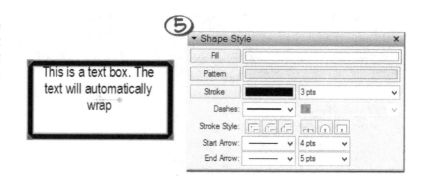

5. To add a border, fill, or other element property, use the **Shape Style panel** while the text box is selected. (**Figure 3-74**)

This type of text is called a **bounded text box**, because the area of text is bounded to a predefined area. You can create an unbounded text that does not constrain to a certain area. Just click at the insertion point to insert the text, instead of clicking and dragging to define the boundary.

If you'd like to convert text from bounded to unbounded after it has been created, right click on the text, and select **Make Bounded**, or **Make Unbounded** from the context menu.

Auto-Text

Auto-Text lets you insert tags inside text boxes that display the tag's predefined value. For example, if you used the Auto-Text tag **<PageNumber>**, the text would show the page number of the page that text box is on.

To insert a <PageNumber> Auto-Text tag, follow these steps: (Figure 3-76)

1. Use the Text Tool (T) to insert a text box.

2. Inside the text box, type <PageNumber>. Auto-Text Tags are case sensitive, so make sure you capitalize them properly. You

can also insert Auto-text tags from a menu by going to **Text ->**
Insert AutoText -> then selecting the Autotext tag you'd like to
insert. (**Figure 3-75**)

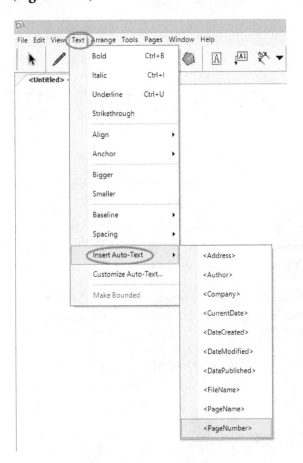

Figure 3-75
Insert Auto Text
from a menu
while entering
text.

3. Press ESC to finish editing the text box.

4. The tag <PageNumber> will automatically change to display
the page number of the page you inserted the text box onto.

Auto-Text tags are dynamic, meaning that they update automatically when their values change. The benefit to this is that you don't ever have to worry about updating them individually.

If you were to copy and paste the **<PageNumber>** Auto-Text box to another page, it would automatically update to display the new page number.

There are a number of special types of Auto-Text tags you can use in LayOut document that will display predefined values. (You can also create custom tags that display text that you define.)

- ✓ Page Number

- ✓ Page Name

- ✓ File Name

- ✓ Current Date

- ✓ Date Created

- ✓ Date Modified

- ✓ Date Published

To view all the Auto-Text tags in your document, go to **File -> Document Setup -> Auto-Text.** In the Document Setup window, you'll see all the preset Auto-Text tags that you can use in your document, and you can edit existing tags or create new ones as well.

Creating a new Auto-Text Tag.

To create a new Auto-Text Tag, follow these steps: (Figure 3-77)

1. Go to **File -> Document Setup -> Auto-Text** to open the Document Setup window.

2. Click the plus icon [+] to create a new tag.

3. Select an Auto-Text value type from the fly-out menu. Custom Text will allow you to define your own tag value, while all the other options will display a preset fixed value.

4. Type in a name for your tag, then press **Enter.** (Just remember that Auto-Text is case sensitive. Also, every tag starts with < and ends with >. If you forget to put them in, it will do it automatically for you.)

5. If you created a custom text tag, type in the text you want displayed into the text box. Otherwise, the other types of Auto-Text may or may not have some settings that you can adjust to change the way the text looks.

Figure 3-77
Creating a new
Auto-Text tag.

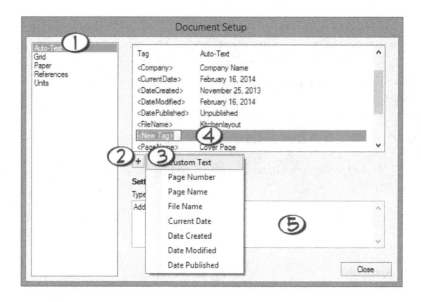

Using Auto-Text

There are plenty of different uses for Auto-Text. Here are some examples on how Auto-Text can make your workflow a lot faster:

✓ **Page Numbers** - If you've been using LayOut for any length of time, you know how frustrating it is to have to update your page numbers whenever you add more pages to your documents. Use the <PageNumber> Auto-Text Tag for the page numbers displayed on each page, and update the elements in your scrapbook wherever they reference page numbers.

✓ **Page Name** - Now, you can link the page name you set in the Pages panel to an Auto-Text tag in your document. Whenever you update the name of the page in the Pages panel, the Auto-Text tag will update.

✓ **Customer & Job Info** - When you create your titleblock template, use custom Auto-Text Tags for all customer and job information. For each new project, instead of manually unlocking the titleblock layer and editing each text block, you'll just open the Document Setup window and change the value of each custom Auto-Text tag. Create your own Auto-Text Tags such as <CustomerName>, <CustomerAddress>, <JobName>, <JobAddress>, <JobNumber>

✓ **Dates & Revisions** - Using the various built-in date Auto-Text values, you can insert tags for date created, date modified, date published, or current date. This is useful for tracking and displaying revision history.

✓ **Combining Auto-Text** - When you use Auto-Text, you can combine tags with other text or tags, all within the same text box. So you could have a text box with "<FileName> was first created on <DateCreated>".

Text with Leader

If you want to add a note and have a leader line pointing at something, LayOut has a special tool called the **Label tool,** made just for that. The great thing is that the leader stays connected to the text box, making repositioning very easy.

To add a text with leader, activate the layer you'd like to add the label to, activate the Label tool and follow these steps: (Figure 3-78)

Step by Step

1. Click once at the endpoint of the leader.

2. Double click at the point where you'd like your text.

3. Type your text, press ESC to finish.

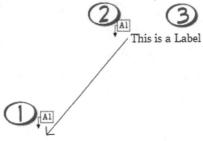

Figure 3-78
Insert a label.

Custom Leaders

There are a number of ways to customize the look of your leader lines. You can make your leader lines curved, for instance. One of the reasons curved leader lines are so nice is that they are less likely to be confused with lines occurring in your viewport. This makes your overall document easier to understand.

LayOut 2015 changed the way leader lines can be drawn. The way your leader lines appear depends upon how you click at the endpoint of the leader and the insertion point of the text (**Figure 3-79**). As you know, to insert a straight leader, click once at the endpoint then double click at the text insertion point.

For curved leaders you can click and drag, or you can insert a two-segmented leader by clicking three points. See below for all options.

Figure 3-79 You can customize the way your leader lines look depending upon how you click.

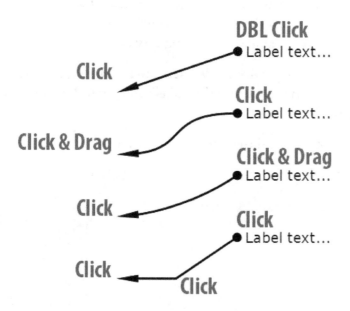

Smart Labels

When you anchor a label to a SketchUp object in a viewport, the **Label tool** will pre-populate its text with data from that object (LayOut 2015). The type of data that will be available to the Label tool depends upon what type of object you click on. It's just like the Auto-text tool, except the text data is pulled from objects in your model. Some examples of data are:

✓ **Group Name, Component Definition** - You can choose to display the name of any of the groups or parent groups of the object you anchor the label to.

✓ **Length, Area, Volume, Coordinates** - The label tool can pull various measurements from the object. If you anchor to an edge, you can read it's length. If you anchor to a face, you can read it's area. Solid groups and components will be able to give you volume. Snapping to points will extract its coordinates.

✓ **Dynamic Component Attributes** ▶ - If you anchor to a dynamic component, you'll see DC attributes indicated by an icon ▶. This provides incredible power to pull data from your model. Although beyond the scope of this book, Dynamic Components allow you to create values related to a components' size, position, rotation, material, or any other custom attribute you define.

✓ **Classifications** ◆ - Tagging objects in your model with the Classifier tool will allow you to add attributes to components based off of a predefined schema. Classifications are indicated by the tag icon ◆.

Now that this tool is available in LayOut, you should approach things differently in SketchUp. Think about your group/component naming, organization and structure, as they have an effect on what text will be available in the Label tool. If you'd like additional data attached to objects in your model, consider using Dynamic Component Attributes or Classifications.

Step by Step

To create a new Smart Label, follow these steps:

1. Activate the Label tool. A1

2. Hover over an object in a viewport. Notice how the cursor snaps to edges, faces, and points in the viewport. Click on an object in order to anchor the label leader line and read its attributes.

3. Double-click where you want the text to be placed, and you'll see the label prepopulate with one of the attributes.

4. To choose which data you'd like to read, click on the arrow to bring up the Label text window.

5. The Label text window has two columns. The left column allows you to select which entity you'd like to read data from. This will start with the entity you've snapped to, whether it's an edge, face, or end point (Vertex), and it will include a group and any parent groups that entity belongs to. Select which entity you'd like to read data from.

6. The right column will display the available values you can place in the label text. Different types of values will be available depending upon what type of entity you've selected. Double-click on the value you'd like to place in the text.

7. Press ESC to accept the auto-text.

Figure 3-80
Choose the entity and the auto-text you'd like to display in the label.

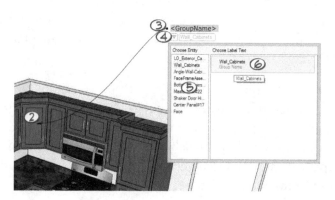

Chapter Summary

✓ Overset text will show a red arrow to let you know you need to increase the size of the bounding box.

✓ Labels can have straight, curved leaders, or two-segmented leaders.

✓ Labels anchored to models in viewports can extract data from your model and display it as auto-text.

Patterns/Hatching

Patterns were introduced in LayOut 2013 to give you the ability to add tiled pattern fills to **shape elements** in LayOut.

In order to insert a pattern, you must first have a shape element to apply it to. You cannot apply a pattern directly to a SketchUp model viewport, you must first trace over it with one of the shape tools.

To create a shape and apply a pattern to it, activate the layer you'd like to add the shape to, activate the drawing tool you'd like, and follow these steps: (Figure 3-81)

Figure 3-81
Apply patterns to
shape elements
in LayOut.

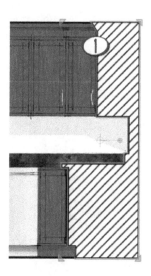

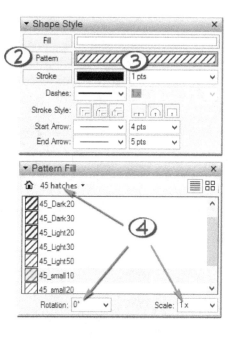

Step by Step

1. Use the shape tools to create a shape on top of your viewport.

2. With the shape selected, click the **Pattern button** to add a pattern to it.

master**Sketchup**.com

3. Double-click the pattern swatch to change the pattern style.

4. In the **Pattern Fill panel**, select the pattern you want and adjust the rotation and the scale.

Alternatively, you can quickly apply patterns to shapes already drawn by clicking and dragging them directly from the **Pattern Fill panel** onto the shape.

Exploding Viewports

You can explode vector viewports by right-clicking them and selecting explode. This will turn it into a LayOut shape element, but if it's a complicated shape it may not convert correctly.

If it doesn't convert correctly, you won't be able to apply a pattern to it, and you will also lose any dynamic link with your SketchUp model so I don't recommend it.

Chapter Summary

✓ You can only add patterns to LayOut shape elements.

✓ Although you can explode viewports to apply patterns to the resulting shape, it is not recommended.

Scrapbooks

What component libraries do for SketchUp, scrapbooks do for LayOut. Scrapbooks are collections of commonly used notes, annotations, and symbols, that you can easily drag and drop into your LayOut documents.

Scrapbooks also act as a style pallet, allowing you to use the **Style tool (B)** to sample any element in it to quickly apply style changes to tools and elements in LayOut.

Scrapbook Elements

Scrapbooks are simply LayOut documents that have various elements on them arranged in a way that makes it easy to select or sample from the **Scrapbook panel**. You can create your own or customize the default scrapbooks that are included with LayOut.

To insert a scrapbook element onto a page in LayOut, follow these steps: (Figure 3-82)

Figure 3-82
LayOut has a number of built-in scrapbooks to choose elements from.

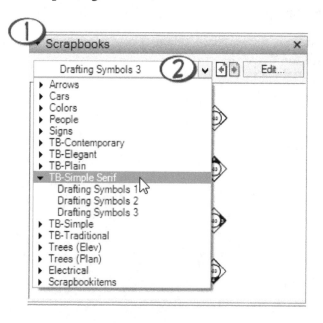

1. Expand the **Scrapbooks panel**.

2. Browse the library of scrapbooks from the dropdown menu. Select a scrapbook.

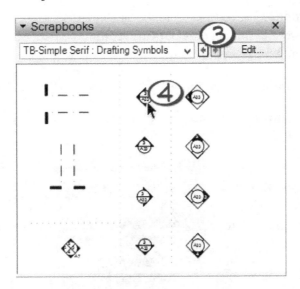

Figure 3-83
Pick a scrapbook element you'd like to place into your document.

3. Click the forward and back buttons to browse each page of the scrapbook document. (**Figure 3-83**)

4. When you find an element you'd like to insert, click on the element with the **Select tool (Spacebar)**. This will turn the **Select tool** into a sort of "stamp" tool.

5. Click on the page wherever you'd like to place the element.

6. You can continue to place copies of the element, or press spacebar or ESC to exit the stamp mode.

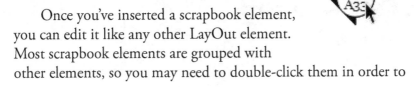

Once you've inserted a scrapbook element, you can edit it like any other LayOut element. Most scrapbook elements are grouped with other elements, so you may need to double-click them in order to edit the individual entities.

Scrapbook Sampling

You don't have to insert scrapbook elements into your model in order to get the full benefits of using scrapbooks. They are actually really handy for sampling styles you've set up as scrapbook items.

To sample a tool style, follow these steps: (Figure 3-84)

1. Select any drawing tool. For example, the **Line tool (L).**

2. Hover over the **Scrapbook panel.** Notice how the cursor changes to an eyedropper.

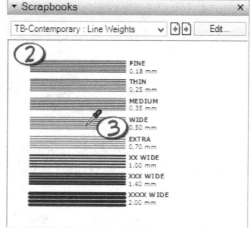

3. Click on any element in the scrapbook to sample its style and apply it to the active tool.

4. Draw an element. The tool will draw in the same style as the sampled scrapbook item.

Figure 3-84 You can sample style settings from your scrapbook elements.

To change an existing element's style to match the style of a scrapbook item, follow these steps:

1. Activate the **Style tool (S).**

2. Click on the scrapbook item you'd like to sample.

3. Click on the element you'd like to change. (Notice the cursor changes to a paint bucket.)

Custom Scrapbooks

Scrapbooks are actually LayOut documents that have been earmarked to show up in the **Scrapbooks panel**. You can edit them by selecting a scrapbook from the **Scrapbooks panel**, and clicking **Edit**.

To add a folder to the Scrapbook panel so you can create your own scrapbooks, follow these steps: (Figure 3-85)

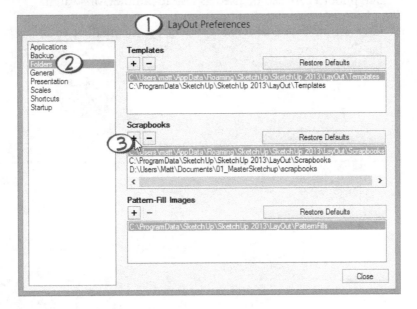

Figure 3-85 Add custom folders to your scrapbooks.

1. Go to **Edit -> Preferences**.

2. Select the **Folders window**.

3. Under **Scrapbooks**, click the plus sign to add a folder to the scrapbook collection.

4. Add LayOut documents with your scrapbook items to that folder, and they will show up in the **Scrapbooks panel** in

Step by Step

LayOut.

When you create scrapbook documents, make sure you group your elements together so they can be sampled as a complete element. Also, make sure you lock layers that you don't want to be able to sample from.

Chapter Summary

✓ Scrapbooks can help you insert commonly used elements into your LayOut document.

✓ Scrapbooks can also be used as a style sampler, or swatch.

✓ Create your own custom scrapbooks for use in all of your LayOut documents.

Printing/Presentation

LayOut has numerous export capabilities that are fairly straight forward. It also has a built-in interactive presentation tool that is great for showing off your LayOut document. We'll go over a few of the basic export features.

Printing

When you created your LayOut document, you should have selected the correct paper size that matches the paper you are going to be printing on.

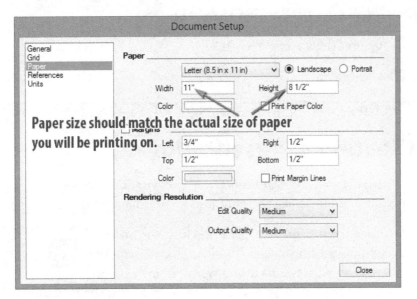

Figure 3-86
Document Setup paper size.

You can confirm these settings by going to **File -> Document Setup**. (**Figure 3-86**) If you need to change the paper size you can do it here and all the pages in your document will resize. Your titleblock elements will not likely be the correct size after the change so it's important to make sure you are working on the correct size when you start a new document.

If you have set your viewport scales and have selected the correct paper size, you will be able to **print your document to accurate scale by following these steps:**

1. Go to **File -> Print.**

2. Select your printer.

3. Click Print.

Exporting PDF

LayOut has a built-in PDF exporter for creating PDF files of your document.

To create a PDF, follow these steps:

1. Go to **File -> Export -> PDF.**

2. Create a file name and click **Save.**

3. Verify the settings, select an output quality, then click **Export.**

Creating a Presentation

LayOut has a built-in full-screen presentation tool for performing full-screen presentations of your LayOut document.

To enter presentation mode, click on the **Start Presentation button** on the toolbar. The presentation will start on whatever page you were currently on, so make sure to go to page one if you want to start at the beginning.

✓ **Left-click** - Advance forward one page

✓ **Right-click** - Move backward one page

✓ **Drag mouse** - Draw on screen or make notes

✓ **Double-click model** - Enter orbit mode to navigate the model in 3D during your presentation.

✓ **Right-click in model space** - Change camera tool, or play animation of model.

Perform a presentation in person, or use a tool like join. me, Google Hangout, or www.gotomeeting.com to share your presentation live over the internet.

Chapter Summary

✓ LayOut makes it very easy to print to scale as long as you properly set up your page size when you create your document.

✓ Send your construction documents electronically by exporting a PDF from LayOut.

✓ Perform a live presentation of your document directly from LayOut.

Hatching Techniques

One important technique used in construction documents is to apply a hatch or pattern to areas in your drawings. They can help identify materials, spaces, and objects that are cut by a section plane.

There are numerous ways to apply hatching in your construction documents: some ways using SketchUp, while others can be done in LayOut.

Solid Black Poché

If you want to show off a perspective view of your model but don't want to see the inside of objects that have been cut by a section plane, use this method to create the illusion of a poché fill. (**Figure 4-1**)

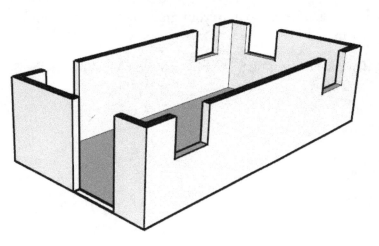

Figure 4-1 Solid Black poché fill applied to a section cut model.

Simply paint the inside faces of your model in SketchUp to match the color of your edges and section cut lines (typically black). This will disguise the edges inside your model, giving the illusion that a solid black face has been created at the section cut.

To create a solid black poché in SketchUp, follow these steps: (Figure 4-2, Figure 4-3)

Figure 4-2 Insert a section plane.

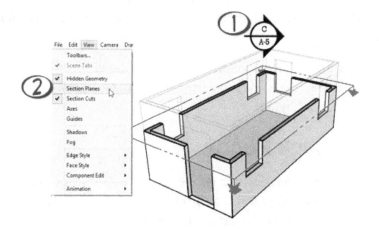

Step by Step

1. Create a section cut of your model using the **Section Plane tool**.

2. Hide the section plane object by going to **View -> Section Planes.**

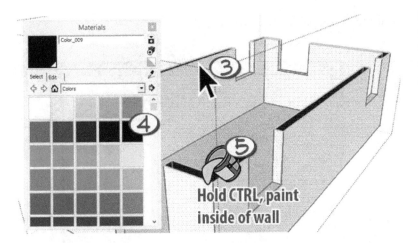

Figure 4-3 Paint the back edges of the model black to disguise the edges.

3. Open the object group by double-clicking on it with the **Select tool (spacebar)**. Select all entities of the group by triple-clicking on the object. (All entities should be highlighted blue.)

4. Activate the **Paint Bucket tool (B)** and select the color **black** from the **Materials window**.

5. Hold down the **CTRL key (Option on Mac)** and click on one of the inner surfaces to paint all similar colors black.

You can use a different color, but it won't disguise the edges so the illusion won't have the same effect.

TIPS Another way to create this poché effect is to create a custom style that changes the default back face color to black. This will prevent you from having to change the colors of the faces. You can find the Back Face setting in the **Styles window -> Edit -> Face Settings -> Back Color**.

Parallel Perspective Hatching

One way to create hatching in a section cut of an object is to paint the inside face of that object in SketchUp with a solid color or hatch texture. Painting the inside face of the object will only expose the texture when showing a section cut. Otherwise, it will

be hidden from view. (**Figure 4-4**)

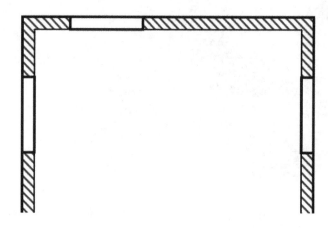

This technique only works in **Parallel Perspective mode**, and when no other paths intersect with the view of the back face. An ideal situation to use this trick is in plan view of a wall.

To create a parallel perspective hatching in SketchUp, follow these steps:

1. Create a section cut of the walls through the doors and windows (**Figure 4-5**).

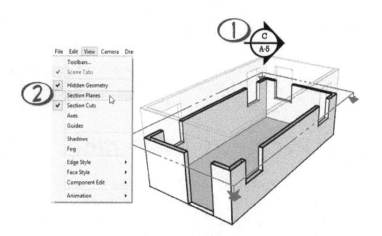

2. Hide the section plane by going to **View -> Section Plane**

3. Go to the **Camera menu** and make sure **Parallel Projection** is selected.

4. Go to **Camera -> Standard Views -> Top** to orient the camera above the walls.

5. With the **Select tool (Spacebar)**, open the walls group by double-clicking on it.

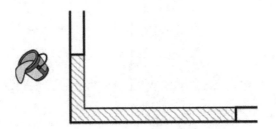

Figure 4-6 Apply hatch texture to back face of model.

6. Apply a hatch texture to the bottom face in the group with the **Paint Bucket tool (B)**. Try using the material named "Sketchy_Lines_Wavy_45_A" located in the "Sketchy" collection in the **Materials window** drop down menu (**Figure 4-6**).

SketchUp doesn't come with any textures that really look like a hatch pattern. If you purchased the Professional package when you bought this book, you will have access to a library of hatch patterns created specifically for this purpose. If you would like to purchase the Professional package separately, you can find it at www.SketchuptoLayout.com/bonuspacks

Scaling Hatch Patterns

One of the drawbacks of creating hatching in this way is that the hatch does not scale automatically. But you can still change the scale manually by editing the material.

To scale the pattern of a SketchUp material, follow these steps: (Figure 4-7)

Figure 4-7 Scale the material from the **Materials window** in SketchUp.

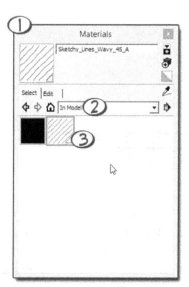
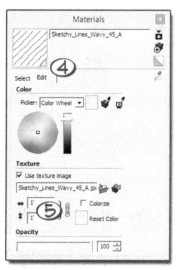

1. Go to **Window -> Materials** to open the **Materials window.**

2. In the **Select tab**, select **In Model** from the drop down menu. This will show you all the different materials in your model.

3. Select the hatch material you need to scale.

4. Click on the **Edit tab** to edit the selected material.

5. Change the scale by typing in a different length for the height and width of the image.

A textured material is just an image that is tiled and repeated across the face of an object. By changing the size of the material, you are defining how big each textured image should be in relationship to the scale of the model.

TIP If you want to use the same material in your model more than once at different scales, you must create a new material for each one. In the **Materials window**, just click the "Add Material button" located at the top right side of the window. Don't forget to label your materials so you can easily identify them later.

Whether you create hatch patterns in LayOut or SketchUp, both of them use raster images to create hatches. So that shouldn't affect your decision over which program you should use to create hatches in.

The drawback to creating hatches in LayOut is that hatches can only be applied to shapes and elements created in LayOut. If you make any changes to your model in SketchUp, those changes will also have to be duplicated manually to the hatched elements in LayOut.

Textured Poché Fills

It is possible to create a solid surface wherever a section plane intersects with your model in order to apply a hatching pattern to it. (**Figure 4-8**)

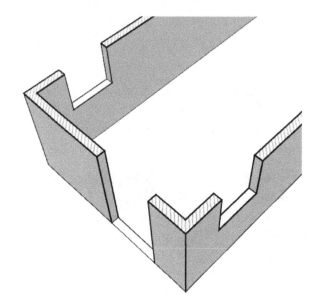

This method creates a set of entities by using the **Create Group from Slice** operation in SketchUp. This step by step method assumes you've already created a section cut plane through your model.

To create a textured poche fill, create a section cut through your model and follow these steps: (Figure 4-9)

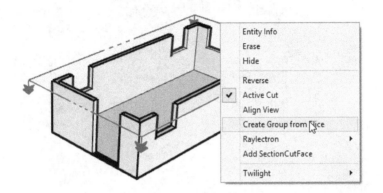

1. Right-click on the section plane object (Make sure the section plane object is visible. Go to **View -> Section Planes** if it's not), select **Create Group From Slice. (Figure 4-9)**.

This will create a new group of edges wherever the section plane intersects with your model. Your original model remains unharmed because this new linework is created in its own, new group.

Next, we need to isolate your new linework group from the active section cut, because right now your new group is being hidden by the active section cut. You can do this by grouping the section cut with your main model, leaving the linework outside of this group. (**Figure 4-10**)

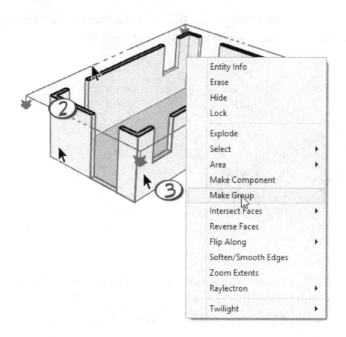

2.   Select the section plane object and the main model.

3.   Group them together by **right-clicking -> Make Group**.

When you **Create Group from Slice**, SketchUp will automatically group the linework based upon the objects that were sliced. Usually, you'll want to explode all of the subgroups in your linework so you can edit the linework from within one group, as opposed to multiple sub-groups.

An easy way to find out if there are subgroups in the linework group is to look for them in the **Outliner window**.

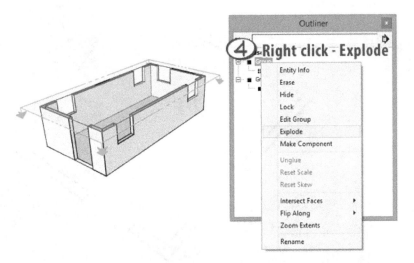

Figure 4-11
Explode any subgroups in the linework group from the **Outliner window**.

4. Go to **Window -> Outliner** to view the group structure of your model. Right-click and explode all the subgroups of your new group until you're left with one group containing all the linework. (**Figure 4-11**)

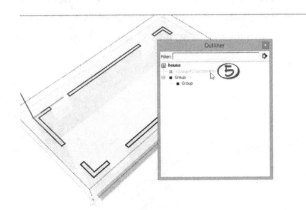

Figure 4-12
Open the linework group from the **Outliner window**.

5. Double-click the linework group in the Outliner to open it for editing. (**Figure 4-12**).

6. Go to **View -> Component Edit -> Hide Rest of Model**, to hide objects not currently being edited. This makes it easier to edit the linework group since its location is within the walls of the main model.

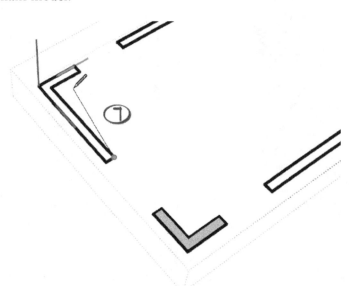

7. Use the **Select tool (Spacebar)** to highlight one of the edges in the linework group in order to verify you are indeed editing the entities in the group. With the **Line tool (L)**, retrace over one edge in each object to make a face appear within (**Figure 4-13**).

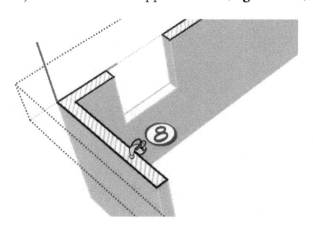

8. Use the **Paint Bucket tool (B)** to apply a desired hatch material or color to the faces. (**Figure 4-14**)

9. Use the **Select tool (Spacebar)** and click once outside the group to close it from editing.

The key to this method is staying organized. You might want to assign the section cut group to a layer specifically for that scene, so it only appears when you are viewing that section cut.

You may also want to hide all the edges of the section cut group so they don't bleed through the other faces.

It may also be helpful to turn the section cut group into a component, then make a copy of it somewhere above your model. This makes it easier to manipulate when you have to make modifications to it later on because you won't have the model in your way and you'll be able to select it easier.

SectionCutFace Plugin

If you liked the previous method of creating poché fills, but didn't like having to manually retrace all of the edges, there is a great plugin called **SectionCutFace** that automates the process for you.

This free plugin is made by TIG, and can be found downloaded using the free Sketchucation plugin manager.

Go to sketchucation.com/pluginstore to download.

When you have the plugin installed, you just right-click any section plane object, click "Add Section Face" and a window will pop up. (**Figure 4-15**)

Figure 4-15
SectionCutFace
plugin by TIG
creates faces
from section cuts
automatically.

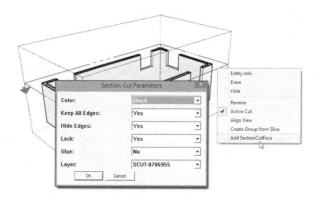

You select the preferred color, whether you want to keep or hide all the edges, the layer to put the group on, and whether you want to lock its position once it's placed.

Click OK and the new group is created with all the parameters you set in the previous window. It's a great tool to have if you like creating section cuts in this manner.

Auto-Scaling Hatching

This method of hatching is accomplished with a style, so no alterations of your model are needed. It also keeps the hatch pattern at a consistent size, no matter what scale you set your viewport to in LayOut. Credit goes to Michael Brightman, author of "The SketchUp Workflow for Architecture" for this method.

The biggest drawback is that it affects everything visible in the model. This forces you to separate objects on different layers in order to control their visibility. You will also have to overlay viewports in LayOut in order to assemble your documents.

Here's how you set up the style to create this effect. You will need to have a black & white inverted tiled image pattern, similar to the image to the right .

**To create a auto-scaling hatch style, follow these steps:
(Figure 4-16)**

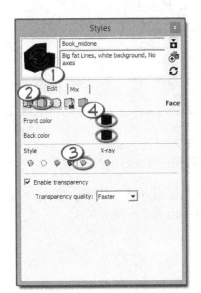 

Figure 4-16 Set the face colors to black, set the background to white.

1. Go to **Window -> Styles** window. Click the **Edit tab.**

2. Select the Face Settings.

3. For Style, choose "Display shaded using all same".

4. Change the front and back color to black, or another grayscale color. (This will make your entire model turn black.)

5. Click on the background settings and change the background to white, turn off Sky and Ground.

6. Click on Watermarks, and click on the plus sign to add a new watermark.

7. Navigate to the image and click OK.

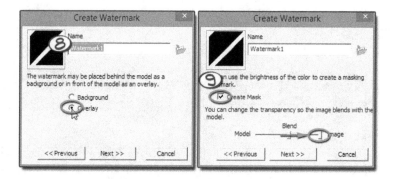

8. In the next window, type in a name for the watermark, and select overlay. Click Next. (**Figure 4-17**)

9. Check the box "Create Mask", and move the Blend slider all the way to the right towards "Image". Click Next.

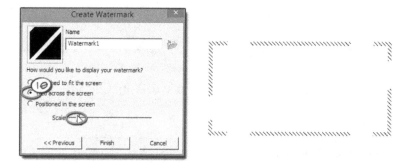

10. Select "Tiled across the screen", and adjust the scale according to your preference. Click Finish. (**Figure 4-18**)

The result is a model completely filled with a hatch pattern. There won't be any edges shown, so this has to be inserted into LayOut underneath another viewport of your model that shows the edges. You are also forced to properly hide objects you don't want hatched by hiding their layers. Otherwise they will show up too.

The biggest advantage to using this approach is that it creates a continuous link between SketchUp and LayOut. Whenever you make a change to your SketchUp model, all you have to do is click "Update reference" in LayOut and the changes will update automatically.

The disadvantage is that it only works correctly in certain camera perspectives, and you are required to stack viewports and separate objects on different layers in order to isolate the objects to apply the hatch style to.

If you take the time to set up your scenes using methods like this, it will save you time down the road.

If you purchased the Professional package, you'll find numerous custom hatch styles that will let you apply CAD type hatch styles to your model. There are also a few styles that create a dashed line effect.

Chapter Summary

✓ Create a solid black poché effect by painting the inside faces of your model black and activating a section plane.

✓ Create a textured hatch by painting the inside faces of your model while in parallel perspective mode and with an active section plane.

✓ Creating a group from a section plane will allow you to create entities that you can apply a hatch material to.

✓ Use the **SectionCutFace** plugin to automate the process of generating entities from section planes.

✓ Create automatically scaling hatching with a custom style that uses watermarks to simulate a hatch pattern.

Stacking Viewports

Sometimes when trying to create scenes for LayOut, it's hard to create something that includes all of the elements you want to display on the page. Even after setting your foreground depth, background depth, and visible objects using SketchUp layers, you might not end up with exactly what you want.

Stacking viewports can provide the flexibility and control you need to create the look you want. (**Figure 4-19**)

Figure 4-19
Stacking viewports gives you greater flexibility with the style of different elements in your model.

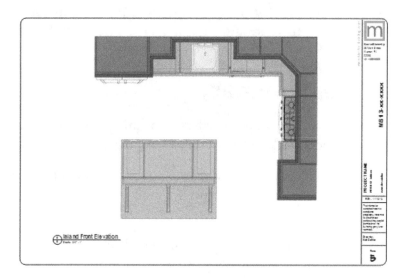

✓ Section cuts actually expose the inside faces of your model wherever they cut away at it. In reality, you might want to stack either a solid or hatched pattern shape or viewport on top of section cuts.

✓ Picking points to dimension from can be challenging in complex models because LayOut is given so many points to pick from. Separating simplified linework allows you to hide the complex viewport while you create dimensions on the simple one.

✓ Separating your linework from your model allows you to render the linework separately. You will then be able to render the main model as raster, and your linework as vector, making your linework appear sharper without sacrificing performance.

✓ LayOut gives you control over lineweight of edges in your viewports. Creating multiple sets of viewports gives you even more flexibility to assign different lineweights to different elements of your model.

As an example, many times you want to show a colorful rendered model in plan view, but want to have crisp vector lines shown for your wall locations. You can't do this in just one viewport.

An easy way to add this flexibility to your LayOut documents is to stack multiple viewports on top of each other. The viewports will have the same scene perspective (Camera location, perspective, scale, etc.), but will have different styles applied and different visible objects shown.

Step by Step

To create a set of stacked viewports, follow these steps:

1. In SketchUp, create two different scenes, both with the same camera settings and perspective, but different styles and visible layers. (**Figure 4-20**)

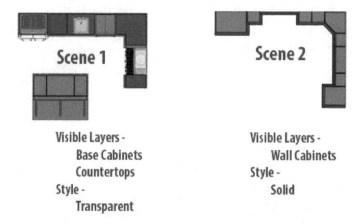

In this model, I wanted to see the base cabinets underneath the countertop so I set a transparent style but I didn't like that the wall cabinets were also transparent. By creating two separate scenes, I'm able to have the transparent style for the base cabinets and countertops, and have a solid style for the wall cabinets.

Figure 4-21 Insert the first viewport into LayOut.

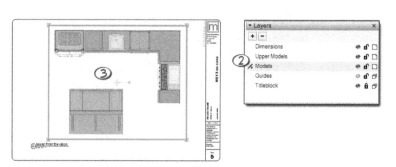

2. In LayOut, activate the layer that you want to insert the first viewport onto. (**Figure 4-21**)

3. Go to **File -> Insert** to insert the SketchUp model. Set the

scene to the one you want for the bottom viewport. Resize
the viewport and set the scale of the model. (For step by step
instructions on inserting a viewport, see the Inserting SketchUp
models chapter.)

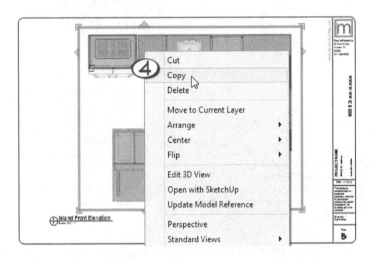

Figure 4-22 Copy
the viewport.

4. Right-click the viewport, and click **Copy. (Figure 4-22)**

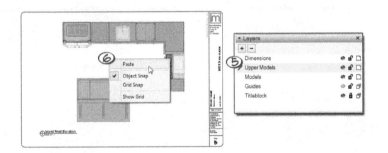

Figure 4-23 Paste
the viewport on a
higher layer.

5. Activate a new layer above the one the first viewport is on.
(**Figure 4-23**)

6. Right-click in the workspace, and click **Paste**.

At this point, you may not notice but you've just pasted a copy
of the same viewport directly on top of the first one. You placed
them on separate layers in order to make it easier to select and edit

them later on.

Figure 4-24
Change the new
viewport to the
second scene.

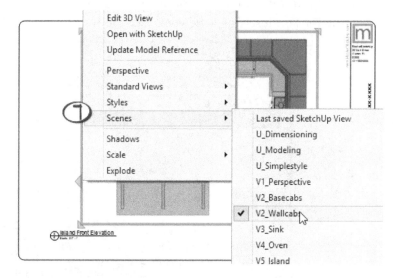

7. Right-click on the newly inserted viewport and select the next scene you prepared to be on top of the first viewport. (**Figure 4-24**)

One common use for stacking viewports is to separate linework from your model, and place that linework on top of a colorful rendered viewport.

Peel Away View

One effect that can be created by stacking viewports is a "peel away view". This creates the illusion that part of the model is being peeled away in order to expose parts underneath. (**Figure 4-25**)

Figure 4-25 Peel away view creates the illusion that part of the model is being peeled away to expose parts underneath.

Create two scenes in SketchUp from the same perspective, but of two different types of content. For example, one scene with framing shown, and another scene fully rendered. Insert these as viewports, one on top of the other, and use a clipping mask to create a peel away view effect.

Place both scenes aligned on top of each other in LayOut, with the framing viewport on top of the fully rendered model viewport.

Figure 4-26
Layer 1 has the
fully rendered
model. Layer 2
has a clipping
mask of the
framing members.

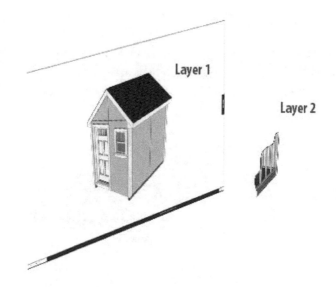

Create a clipping mask over the framing viewport with a corner cut away. This will create the illusion that the sheathing is being peeled away to expose the framing members underneath. (**Figure 4-26**)

Pasting Linework into LayOut

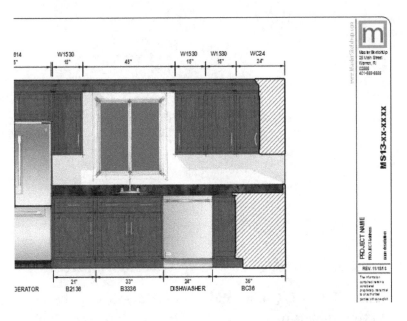

Figure 4-27
Copying and
pasting linework
into LayOut.

Another method to insert a linework viewport into LayOut is to copy and paste. (**Figure 4-27**) By copying and pasting entities directly into LayOut, you eliminate the need to create and manage scenes. However, you lose the dynamic link between your SketchUp model and LayOut, so if you make any updates to your model, you'll have to also copy and paste an updated set of linework as well.

To copy and paste linework into LayOut, follow these steps: (Figure 4-28, Figure 4-29)

1. In SketchUp, create a group from section cut using either the **Textured Poché fills** technique or the **SectionCutFace plugin** as described in a previous chapter.

2. Since we will be pasting the linework into LayOut directly, I like to move the **SectionCutFace** group to the outside of my main model to make it easier to see and select when the section

cut is inactive.

Figure 4-28
Create groups
from section cut,
and copy onto
your clipboard.

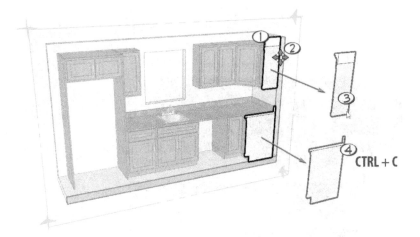

3. Select the linework group with the **Select tool (Spacebar)**.

4. Press **CTRL + C (Command + C on Mac)** to copy the object to your clipboard.

Figure 4-29 Paste
linework into
LayOut, orient
and set scale.

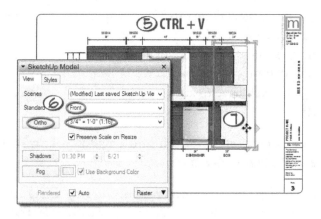

5. In LayOut, navigate to the page where you'd like to place the linework, press **CTRL + V (Command + V on Mac)** to paste the linework into a new viewport on the page.

6. Use the **SketchUp Model panel** to turn on Ortho, orient to a standard view, and set the scale to match the other viewport scale.

7. Position the linework on top of the other viewport.

Just remember that by copying and pasting elements into LayOut like this you have lost any dynamic link to the original SketchUp model in that viewport. If you make any changes to your SketchUp model, you'll have to create another "group from slice" and paste it into LayOut again.

Transparency Between Viewports

In LayOut, you have the ability to control the opacity of your viewports. Well, sort of. Although you can't control the transparency of a viewport or layer directly, you can place a shape element with a white fill over a viewport, and adjust the opacity of the fill of the shape.

Since the shape fill is white, it matches the color of the background paper creating the illusion that you've adjusted the opacity of the viewport beneath it.

You don't have to insert a shape into your model every time you want to mask a viewport. Remember that viewports are considered LayOut elements too, right? That means you can select an overlaid viewport, go to shape style, and add a white fill and adjust the opacity of the viewport's fill to affect the visibility of any viewports underneath it.

To change the opacity of an overlaid viewport, follow these
steps: (Figure 4-30)

Figure 4-30 Add
a fill to an overlaid
viewport, set it to
white and adjust
the opacity to
affect the visibility
of the viewport
underneath.

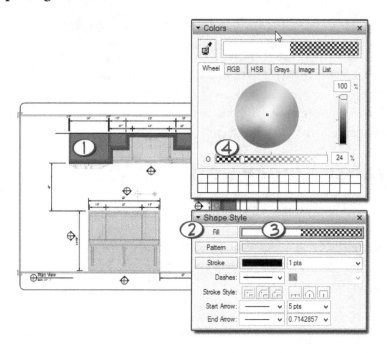

*Step by
Step*

1. In LayOut, select a viewport that is overlaid on top of another
   viewport or element.

2. Open the **Shape Style panel** and activate the **Fill button**.

3. Double-click on the color swatch next to the **Fill button** to
   open the **Colors panel**.

4. Select white, then adjust the transparency slider until you reach
   the transparency level you desire.

Pattern Masks

You can also create unique masking effects using the pattern
fill feature in LayOut. By placing a shape or a viewport on top of
another viewport and applying a tonal pattern to it, you can create
a mask effect on anything underneath it. (**Figure 4-31**)

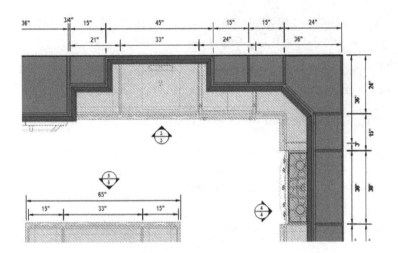

Figure 4-31 Using a white tonal pattern with an overlaid viewport will mask any viewports underneath.

In order for this to work, you'll need to choose any of the patterns labeled "**White**" from the "**Tonal Patterns**" folder in LayOut.

To create a pattern mask over a viewport, follow these steps: (Figure 4-32)

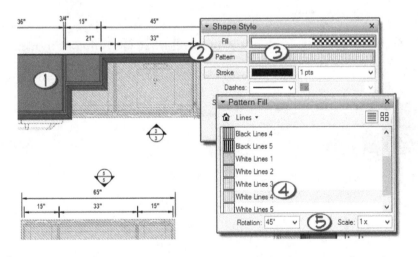

Figure 4-32 Add a pattern to an overlaid viewport.

1. In LayOut, select a viewport that is overlaid on top of another viewport or element.

2. Open the **Shape Style panel** and activate the **Pattern button**.

Step by Step

3. Double-click on the pattern swatch next to the **Pattern button** to open the **Pattern Fill panel**.

4. Navigate to the **Tonal Patterns -> Lines** folder from the drop-down menu. Select one of the patterns labeled **White Lines**.

5. Change the scale and rotation if needed.

You can't change the opacity of patterns in LayOut, but you can import your own custom images that have transparency settings already applied to them as PNG images.

Chapter Summary

✓   Stack viewports on top of each other to create views that would otherwise be complicated to create from a single scene.

✓   Create a linework scene of your model to make it easier to snap to points when creating dimensions.

✓   Create a 2D version for elements that don't render well in perspective view.

✓   Use a clipping mask to create a peel-away view of your model.

✓   Copy linework from your SketchUp model and paste it directly into LayOut.

Project Overview

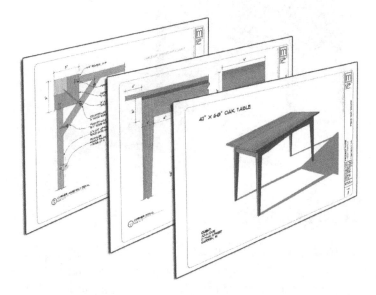

In this simple woodworking table project, we'll go over some modeling techniques and scene preparation methods to help you create stunning shop drawings for your woodworking projects.

✓ Using an Xray style to see through an object

✓ Using Two-Point perspective to prevent vertical warping

✓ Scaling viewports to random scales.

Model Setup

You can follow along with this project by opening the **Table.skp** file that was included in the purchase of this book.

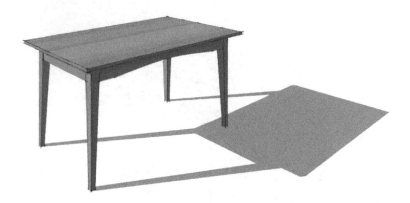

Project Goals

With this project, I wanted to create a highly realistic model of a table. I'm going to model all the joinery and hardware used to build the table. Because it's a relatively small model, I'll also be using high quality wood grain material to enhance the look of my drawings.

The advantage of modeling at this high level of detail is that it forces you to visualize exactly how everything is to be built so you can work out any problems before you actually go to build it.

Layers

I know I've talked a lot about layers in this book, and their importance when trying to control visibility in scenes created for LayOut viewports. So you may be surprised to know that this project has only two layers.

✓ **Layer0**

✓ **TableTop**

The reason I've done this is because the tabletop is the only object in this model that I want to be able to hide in my viewports. Everything else is visible in every viewport so I don't need to spend any time creating layers for them.

As far as keeping organized while modeling, I take advantage of the "hide rest of the model" option available from **View -> Component Edit -> Hide Rest of Model**. This hides other parts of the model while I am editing groups. I even set up a keyboard shortcut for this. If you want to learn how to create custom keyboard shortcuts for yourself, check out my tutorial at www.MasterSketchup.com/sketchup-tutorial-keyboard-shortcuts/

Start Modeling

If you're a beginner and would like a more detailed step by step instructions on how to draw a table, check out my tutorial at www. MasterSketchup.com/modeltable. However, if you have a basic understanding of SketchUp you should be able to follow along with this project.

Table Top

We'll draw the table top first in order to give us a surface to model the rest of the table parts on. (**Figure 5-1**)

1. Use the **Rectangle tool (R)** to draw a rectangle to the size of the table top, 42" x 72".

2. Extrude it with the **Push/Pull tool (P)** to the thickness you need.

Figure 5-1
Draw the table top first.

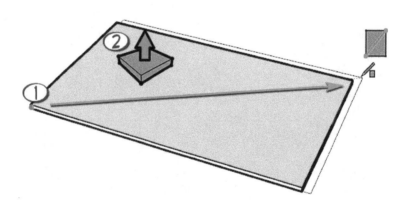

3. Triple-click the table top and turn it into a group to isolate it.

Table Leg

We're going to draw this table upside down, then flip it over when we're all done. It's just easier to see what we're doing from above. (**Figure 5-2**)

1. Draw some guides using the **Tape Measure tool (T)** 4" from the edge of the table to create an intersection point where we will locate one of the table legs.

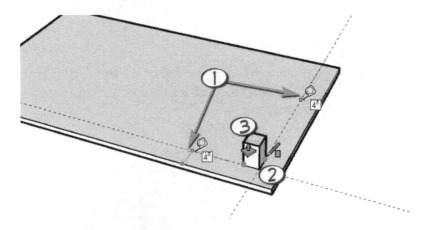

Figure 5-2
Create guides, draw rectangle, and extrude 5" to define point at which the taper begins.

2. Use the **Rectangle tool (R)** to create a 3" x 3" rectangle, starting from the intersection point of the guides.

3. Using the **Push/Pull tool (P)**, extrude the table leg up 5" in order to create edges at the point where the taper will begin.

4. Push/Pull again, but this time, press the **CTRL key (Option key on Mac)** in order to create an additional face and continue to extrude the table leg to 30". The overall length of the leg should be 35". You should also see edges at the 5" height. (**Figure 5-3**)

Figure 5-3
To extrude
an additional
face, tap **CTRL
(Option key
on Mac)** while
using the **Push/
Pull tool (P)**.

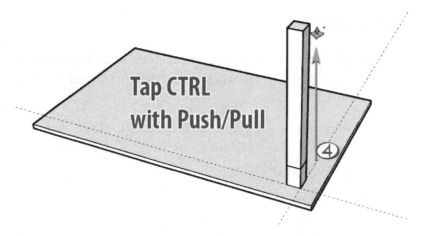

5. Using the **Scale tool (S)**, scale the end of the leg diagonally to a factor of 0.50. This will taper the leg on the two inside edges of the leg. (**Figure 5-4**)

Figure 5-4
Scale the end of
the leg to taper
the sides.

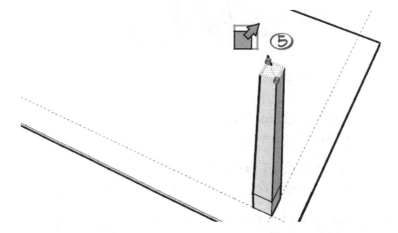

6. Triple-click the leg, and turn it into a component. An exact copy of the leg will be used at the other three corners of the table, so we should use a component instead of a group.

Copy Legs

We still have more detailed work to do on the leg, but sometimes I like to get most of the model roughly drawn before I start spending time on the little details.

We're going to use the same leg component at each corner of the table. Create additional guides if necessary to help you position the legs. Create copies of the leg using the **Move tool (M)** and pressing **CTRL (Option key on Mac)** on your keyboard. Rotate the legs so that the taper is on the interior side of the table. (**Figure 5-5**)

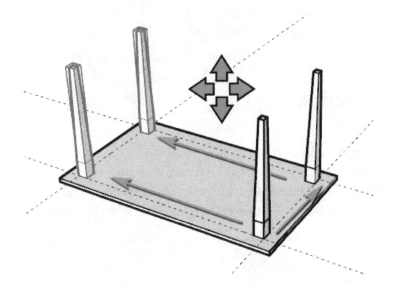

Figure 5-5
Use the **Move tool (M)** to position and rotate the leg components.

Aprons

The aprons are drawn using the **Rectangle tool (R)** and the **Push/Pull tool (P)**. Use components where possible for identical parts. Once you start adding details like joinery, this will save you time from having to do it twice. (**Figure 5-6**)

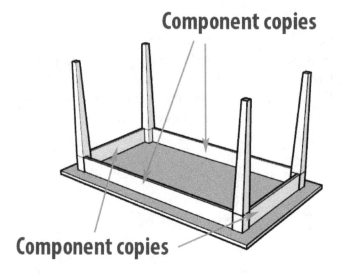

Component copies

Component copies

On the long apron, I have a radius cut out of it. Although
you can use the **Arc tool (A)** built into SketchUp, I used a free
plugin called **BezierSpline** by Fredo. You can download it from the
Sketchucation plugin store at sketchucation.com/pluginstore.

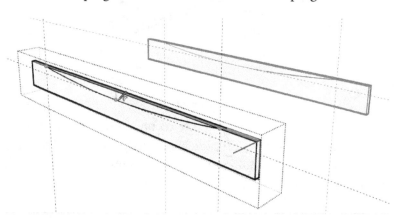

Use the **Tape Measure tool (T)** to create reference lines to help
you snap to points while you draw the arc. (**Figure 5-7**) I created
guides 6" in from each end of the apron, and one 1 1/2" down
from the long edge to snap the radius of the arc to.

Use the **Push/Pull tool (P)** to extrude the arc from the apron.
(**Figure 5-8**)

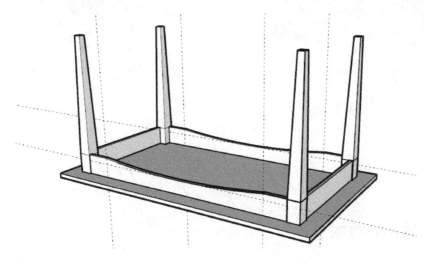

Figure 5-8
Push/Pull tool
(P) is used to
extrude the arc
from the apron.

Details

For a basic set of drawings, the model might be good enough
as is to create drawings from. But I wanted to have a highly
detailed model so I'll add additional details such as the gussets and
hardware. (**Figure 5-9, Figure 5-10**)

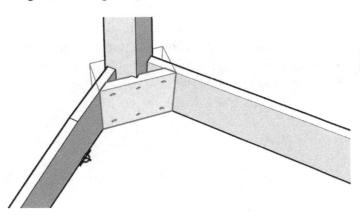

Figure 5-9
Gussets are
inserted with
countersunk
holes.

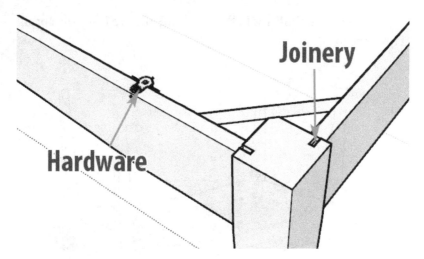

Materials

Because this is such a small model, I can use high quality materials without worrying about slowing down my computer. In this model, I used a high quality custom wood material made from a high resolution scan of a real oak veneer. The advantage of scanning a material versus taking a photograph is that you don't introduce any lens distortion whatsoever into the image. The scan reproduces the oak veneer exactly as it is in real life.

The scanned image was then edited by a professional graphic artist to be completely seamless. This means that the image can be tiled over and over and you won't be able to identify the edge of each image. (**Figure 5-11**)

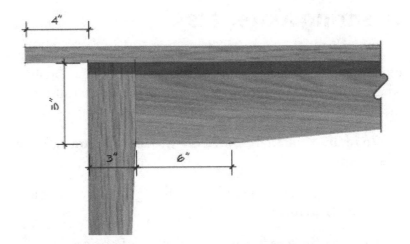

Figure 5-11 High quality material textures make your models look more accurate and professional.

If you purchased the Professional pack with this book, you have access to seven great, high quality wood materials, as well as many more hatch style materials. If you didn't purchase the bonus pack with this book, go to www.Sketchuptolayout.com/bonuspacks to purchase it now. (**Figure 5-12**)

Figure 5-12 These seven high quality real wood materials are available in the Bonus pack.

When painting the faces on this model, you want to paint each individual face, and orient the texture so the grain is running in the correct direction.

Orienting Materials

When you apply a texture directly to a face in your model, you can change the grain direction of the texture. This is important when working with wood textures in order to create a realistic model of your project.

To rotate a material painted on the face of a model, follow these steps:

1. Enter the group you need to edit and right-click on the face you'd like to rotate.

2. Go to the **Texture** fly-out menu and click **Position**. (**Figure 5-13**)

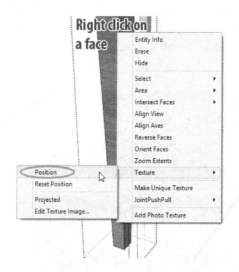

Figure 5-13
Access the
texture
positioning
controls by
right-clicking on
a face.

The full sized texture image will be superimposed over the model and you'll have different controls at each corner that allow you to scale, rotate, skew, distort, and move the image.

3. Click and drag the green control to rotate the image to the correct orientation. (**Figure 5-14**)

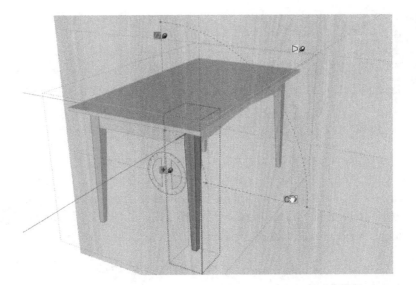

Figure 5-14
The green handle lets you rotate and scale the texture.

Creating Scenes

The process of creating scenes for this model will be very easy because there are no section cuts required. You won't have to worry about hiding and unhiding layers with the exception of one scene where we will hide the table top.

For the most part, all parts of the model will remain visible in each scene. The foreground depth will be determined by the camera location and you don't need to create any section cuts or clipping planes. You also don't need to worry about background depth because we want everything visible in the model.

The only things you'll need to worry about in each scene is camera perspective and style.

Styles

For this project, there are a few different styles I used for modeling, and for setting up the various scenes:

✓ **Modeling** - This is my default modeling style. It has simple, straight edges and fully textured materials. It hides all section plane objects and active cuts by default. This is the style that is active 90% of the time during the process of creating a model.

✓ **Elevations** - This is the style I save with elevation scenes. It's a somewhat sketchy style, but is fully colored and textured. Background is white.

✓ **Xray** - This style is used in the detail view of the leg construction. It allows you to see through the faces of the model.

Utility Scenes

I created a modeling scene that helps me quickly jump back to my preferred settings for modeling, which typically include perspective camera and a basic straight edge style with textures. (**Figure 5-15**)

Figure 5-15
A modeling scene gives you an easy way to jump back to your preferred modeling settings.

I also created two scenes that only saved the axes location, so that I could easily switch between an axis oriented in 45° and one oriented in 90°. (**Figure 5-16**)

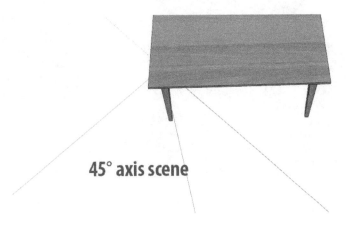

45° axis scene

Figure 5-16
This utility scene saves the axis position only, making it easy to change the inference system when working on 45° angles.

Perspective Scene

On the cover page I want to show a perspective view of the table. When the camera is in perspective mode you'll notice that there is a slight distortion that makes the legs look curved. To counteract that effect, we'll use Two-Point Perspective camera.

Orient your camera to the angle you like, then go to **Camera -> Two-Point Perspective.** Turn on shadows, set the style to a sketchy edge that shows full textures, and save the scene. (**Figure 5-17**)

Figure 5-17
Two_Point Perspective scene set up for the cover sheet.

Perspective No-Top Scene

On the detail page of the drawings, I want to show a perspective view of the table without the table top, so you can see the tabletop hardware and the corner details.

This is the only scene where we need to hide an object. To hide the table top, create a new layer called **TableTop**. Select the table top group and assign it to the **TableTop** layer from the **Entity Info window**.

From the **Layers window**, disable the **TableTop** layer and the table top should disappear.

Orient the camera to the angle you want, and set the camera to Two-Point Perspective. Keep the same sketchy style that you used in the last scene and keep the shadows. (**Figure 5-18**)

Figure 5-18
Two-Point Perspective scene without the top.

Side, Front, Top Scenes

For the viewports that we will be adding dimensions to, we
need to create some scenes that are set to orthogonal perspectives so
that we can set them to specific scales.

Set the camera to parallel perspective. To align the camera
with a surface in your model, right-click on a face and select **Align
View**. Alternatively, use one of the preset camera views in your
toolbar.

Turn on shadows and use a sketchy style to capture this scene.
Create one scene for the front, side, and top of the table. (**Figure
5-19**)

Figure 5-19
The front,
side, and top
scenes are all
set to parallel
projection.

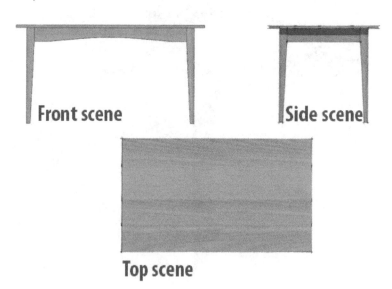

Front scene

Side scene

Top scene

Top Frame Scene

This is the scene that shows all the details on how the table leg is installed, and we will be adding notes identifying all the hardware. This will also be an orthogonal viewport, so we'll need to set the camera to parallel projection.

Orient the camera to a view looking down from above. Hide the table top layer so we can see the joinery and hardware. Zoom in to one of the corner legs. In order to see more of the internal structure of the corner, set the style to one with the Xray setting enabled. (**Figure 5-20**)

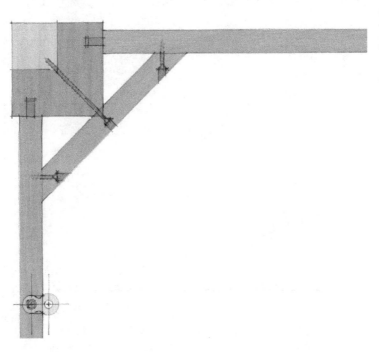

Figure 5-20
This Xray view of the corner let's you see all the screws inside the table.

Export to LayOut

The process of exporting this model to LayOut involves inserting the various viewports and setting them to the appropriate scene. There are no stacked viewports in this project so it should be fairly straight forward.

One thing to keep in mind is the viewports will be set to various scales, so make sure your **Dimension tool (D)** is set to the correct scale when you start to insert dimensions.

Document Template

The document template I used in this project is an 11" x 17" paper (tabloid) size.

Figure 5-21
Table project
LayOut
template.

Cover Page

The cover page will have a perspective view of the table, as well as some customer information. (**Figure 5-22**)

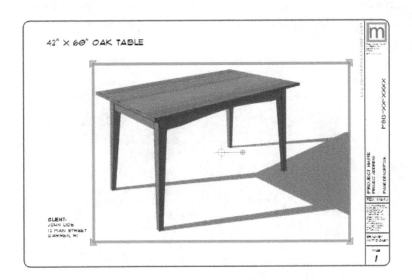

Figure 5-22
Table Cover
Page.

Cover Page Layer Organization

Layer	Contents	Scale
Dimensions	Title, Customer info	N/A
Models	**Perspective**	Perspective
TitleBlock	Titleblock elements	N/A

Elevations Page

The elevations page will have numerous viewports on it. There will be the top, side, and front view of the table. There will also be a copy of the front view inserted and zoomed in so we can add dimensions for the taper and overhang. (**Figure 5-23**)

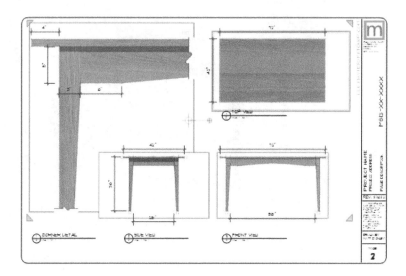

The zoomed in corner detail is set to a non-standard scale of about 1:3.3. You can still add dimensions to a non-standard viewport, you just have to rely on the **Auto Scale** feature in the **Dimension panel** to set the scale accurately.

Elevations Page Layer Organization

Layer	Contents	Scale
Dimensions	Dimensions, annotations	N/A
Models	**Side Parallel, Front Parallel, Top, Front Parallel (zoomed in)**	3/4" = 1'-0", ~1:3.3
TitleBlock	Titleblock elements	N/A

Details Page

The details page has two viewports on it. The perspective view of the table with no top is on the right, and the close up detail of one of the legs is on the left. (**Figure 5-24**)

I couldn't find a standard scale that fit the page well, so I set it to a random scale that I feel provides enough detail of the corner that would allow me to annotate well.

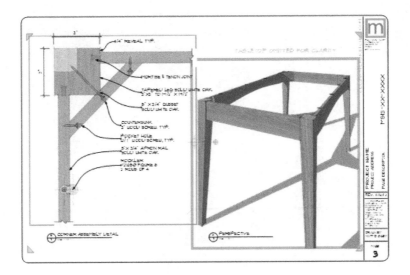

Details Page Layer Organization

Layer	Contents	Scale
Dimensions	Dimensions, annotations	N/A
Models	**topframe, perspectivenotop**	~1:1.53
TitleBlock	Titleblock elements	N/A

Project Overview

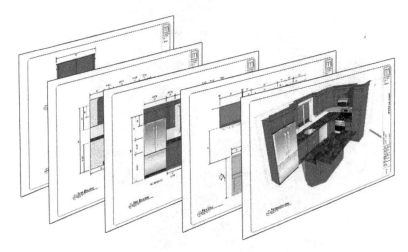

Figure 6-1
Kitchen project
pages.

This is a project that consists of 3D perspective views, elevation and plan views of a kitchen. In this project you'll learn the following:

✓ Organizational methods for a typical kitchen project in SketchUp.

✓ Saving time by using pre-made dynamic cabinet and appliances components.

✓ Use special scenes to create simple versions of viewports to help snap dimensions to.

✓ Create and edit section cuts that can be pasted into LayOut so LayOut patterns can be applied to them.

Model Setup

You can follow along this project by opening the file **Kitchen.skp** that came with your purchase of this book. (**Figure 6-2**)

**Figure 6-2
Kitchen.skp**
model

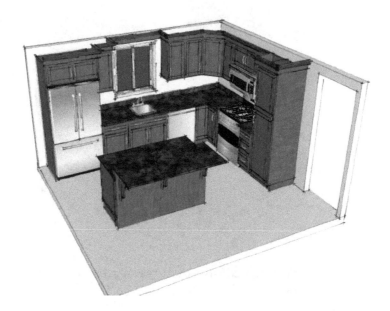

Project Goals

Before starting any project, you'll want to take a look at the big picture and assess your goals for the project. What will this model be used for? By thinking about this now, you'll understand the level of detail that will be required in your model.

Many times when designing a kitchen, you'll create a 3D render of the kitchen as a sales tool in order to win a project. In these situations, the primary purpose of the model is to create a highly detailed **Rendering Model** in order to impress a potential client. Secondary to that is to use the project as a **Coordination Model** to create shop drawings from.

In this situation, you'll focus more on incorporating highly detailed components in your model, complete with photorealistic materials. You'll focus less upon making your model simple, knowing that there may be a little more work involved with dimensioning in LayOut.

Before we start modeling, let's look at a typical organization of a kitchen SketchUp model.

Phase/Location Layer Groups

As you know, you can use groups and components to collect various entities together so they can be manipulated as one assembly. You should also use groups and components to collect similar items together for the purpose of assigning them to a layer.

If your kitchen happens to be a remodeling project, you may want to separate objects into major groups that identify whether they are existing, demolition, or new items. If you are making major structural changes to any walls, you might consider splitting the model into two separate groups that represent each phase.

In this kitchen, we don't have any phases that are applicable to the project, but there are a couple of location layers I am going to implement in order to help keep things organized. (**Figure 6-3**)

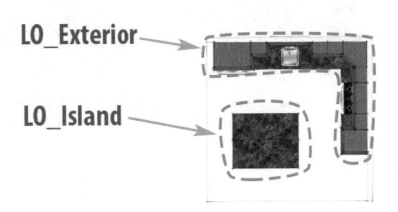

LO_Exterior

LO_Island

Figure 6-3 The kitchen is split into two major location layers.

The kitchen basically consists of two wall elevations, and one island in the center. To make it easier to isolate the island, I'm going to create a layer called **LO_Island** and one called **LO_Exterior Cabinets** to isolate the two locations. There will be two master groups called **Island**, and **Exterior Cabinets** that will contain all the objects for each location. I'll assign those master groups to their appropriate location layers.

Object Layer Groups

Object layers are created to categorize similar objects together, to make it easier to control their visibility throughout the entire project. For this kitchen project, I've created object layers for the following types of objects:

- ✓ **Appliances**

- ✓ **Base Cabinets**

- ✓ **Wall Cabinets**

- ✓ **Countertops**

- ✓ **Floor**

- ✓ **Plumbing**

- ✓ **Trim**

- ✓ **Walls**

- ✓ **Windows**

Within the **LO_Exterior_cabinets** layer group, I have the following object layer groups organizing the various objects: **(Figure 6-4)**

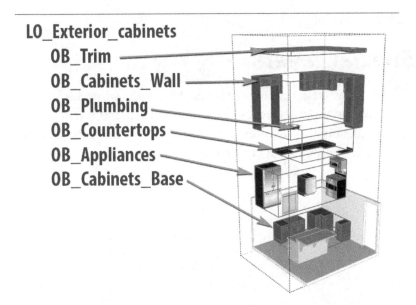

LO_Exterior_cabinets
    OB_Trim
    OB_Cabinets_Wall
    OB_Plumbing
    OB_Countertops
    OB_Appliances
    OB_Cabinets_Base

Figure 6-4
Object layer groups within the exterior cabinet location group.

For the **LO_Island** location group, I've organized the objects onto the following object layers: (**Figure 6-5**)

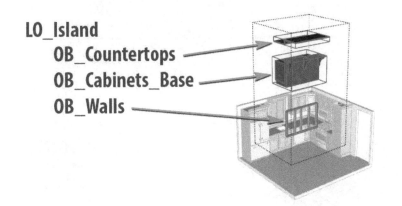

LO_Island
    OB_Countertops
    OB_Cabinets_Base
    OB_Walls

Figure 6-5
Object layer groups within the island location group.

The walls and floor do not reside in either of the location layers. They are just assigned to the object layers **OB_Walls** and **OB_Floor.** You will surely have a different set of layers for your model depending upon the type of project you're working on. Don't expect to know all of the layers you'll need as you begin a project. It's ok to add new layers when you think you need them as you're modeling.

Special Layers

As I was preparing my scenes for LayOut, I created some section cuts and linework, so I created some special layers for them. By doing this, it allows me to only show the section cuts and linework when I am saving a particular scene.

Start Modeling

We will start this kitchen model by creating the walls where the cabinets will be installed.

To begin modeling, start out in a new SketchUp file, and draw a base rectangle and group it in order to give yourself a "floor" to reference off of while modeling. (**Figure 6-6**)

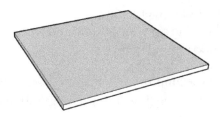

Figure 6-6
Kitchen floor object.

Perimeter Walls

Begin drawing the perimeter of the room using the **Rectangle tool (R)**. Extrude the walls to the height of the ceiling using the **Push/Pull tool (P)**. Add any window and door openings to the walls. Triple-click the wall and make it into a group. (**Figure 6-7**)

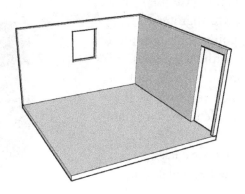

Figure 6-7
Perimeter walls modeled on top of the floor.

Don't worry too much about the thickness of the walls or how they interact with the floor. We will be using a clipping mask in

LayOut around the viewport so they will be hidden anyways.

Cabinets

For kitchens, I recommend using the custom dynamic components from the SketchThis.net plugin. It is a premium plugin, but the different pricing packages allow you to rent short term licenses by the day, or a continuous license if you do kitchens on a regular basis.

By utilizing high quality kitchen cabinet components, you drastically reduce the amount of time and work involved in creating a great kitchen design.

You reduce the amount of actual modeling that is needed and you focus more on dragging and dropping cabinets into different configurations.

Here are some tips for working with cabinets and arranging them in your model:

✓ When you have the **Move tool (M)** active in SketchUp, you can hover over a group or component to reveal handles that allow you to quickly rotate the component. (**Figure 6-8**)

✓ When aligning cabinets, make sure you are aligning the correct points. For instance, on cabinets with face frames, it is common for the side walls of the cabinets to be set back 1/4" from the side of the face frame. Don't try to snap two cabinets together by the back corners, the face frames will end up overlapping.

✓ While moving a cabinet, use the arrow keys to lock axis

references and move the cabinet one axis at a time in multiple steps.

✓ Another advantage to locking axis while moving an object is that you can reference other object inference points in your model to help align things. For example, you can make sure a sink is centered on a cabinet by referencing a midpoint on the cabinet while locking axis during the move.

✓ There are many appliance manufacturers that have their catalog of residential appliances on the 3D warehouse. Take advantage of using the actual appliance you're planning on using in the kitchen in your SketchUp model.

✓ For fillers and other custom accessories, it's ok to draw those manually. Most of the time they are unique objects so they need to be edited anyways.

For this kitchen, I used pre-made cabinet components wherever I could. On each side of the refrigerator, I just drew simple panels that I painted the same material as the cabinets. I also drew the fillers and the kneewall at the island manually. (**Figure 6-9**)

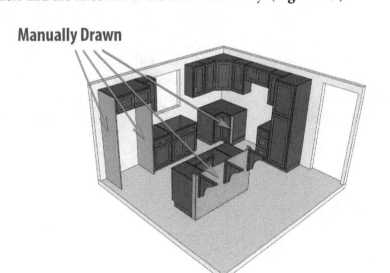

Manually Drawn

Figure 6-9
The only items drawn manually here are the fillers. Everything else is a component from the SketchThis.net library.

For the countertop brackets on the island overhang, I found those on the 3D warehouse as well. You might want to be more accurate by drawing those details manually instead.

Model Organization

At this point, you should have all of your cabinets and fillers positioned in your model. As we said earlier, we want to organize the model onto two different main layers, **LO_Island** and **LO_Exterior_Cabinets**.

Figure 6-10
Create a new group for the island and assign it to the LO_Island Layer.

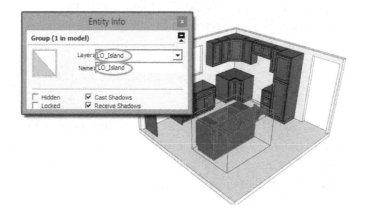

Select all of the cabinets, kneewall, and countertop brackets at the **island**, and **right-click -> Make Group**. Label that group **LO_Island** and assign it to the **LO_Island** layer from the **Entity Info window**. (**Figure 6-10**)

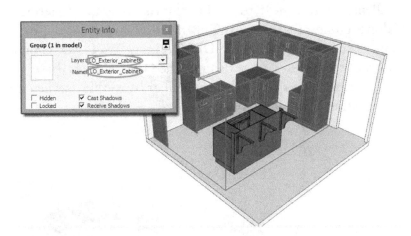

Figure 6-11
Create a new
group for all
the cabinets
on the exterior
walls, and
assign it to the
**LO_Exterior_
Cabinets** layer.

Next, select the rest of the cabinets and fillers on the exterior walls of your model, group them together and name that group **LO_Exterior_Cabinets**. Assign that group to the layer **LO_Exterior_Cabinets** (**Figure 6-11**).

Now that we've defined our **phase/location layer groups,** we can open up each of them and create our **object layer groups**.

Open up the **LO_Island** group, and select all of the cabinets, kneewall, and countertop brackets again. Make those into another group, and assign that group to the object layer **OB_Cabinets_Base**. (**Figure 6-12**)

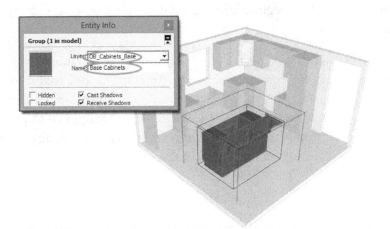

Figure 6-12
Place the Island
cabinets in
another group
and assign it
to the **OB_
Cabinets_Base**
layer.

Repeat these same steps for the cabinets in the **LO_Exterior_ Cabinet** group. (**Figure 6-13**) Only this time, group the upper cabinets and place them on the **OB_Cabinets_Wall** layer. Group the lower cabinets and place them on the **OB_Cabinets_Base** layer. This will let us hide either the wall or base cabinets when we start creating scenes for LayOut.

Figure 6-13
Organize
the exterior
cabinets into
two groups,
one for base
cabinets and
one for wall
cabinets.

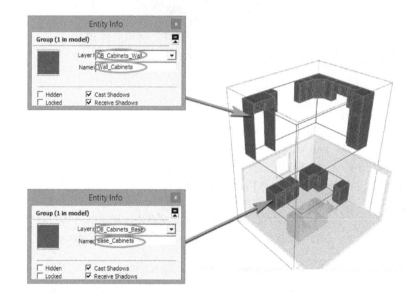

This may seem confusing right now, but it will start to make more sense as we begin adding different types of objects, such as countertops.

You might want to check to make sure you've included everything in the correct layer group. An easy way to check is to hide the layer and if you missed anything, the object will remain visible. In order to move it to the correct layer group, you can drag and drop it from the **Outliner window**, or you can use the cut and "paste in place" method in the Edit menu.

Countertops

I always draw countertops manually. (**Figure 6-14**) The simplest way is to draw a rectangle on the top of a cabinet and use the **Push/Pull tool (P)** to extrude it to the dimensions you need. I find it easier to draw backsplashes in a separate group from the countertops.

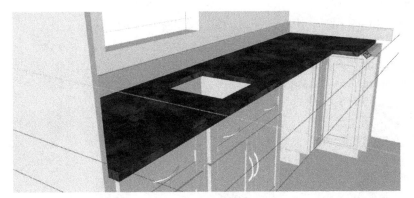

Figure 6-14
Draw the countertops manually, grouping each primitive shape as you go.

Before you start drawing countertops, make sure you are in the appropriate layer group. An easy way to check is to keep the **Outliner window** open. If you are drawing the Island countertops, simply double-click on the **LO_Island** group in the outliner to open it and begin drawing.

Make it a habit to automatically group primitive shapes. So for each "slab" of countertop, triple-click it and turn it into a group. For the island, you'll have a lower countertop and an upper countertop. Each of them should be in their own group. You'll also have the backsplash in its own group. (**Figure 6-15**)

Once you've drawn those three objects, we'll create a new object layer group for countertops at the island. Select the two countertops and the backsplash, and make a group named **Countertops**. Assign that object layer group to the layer **OB_Countertops**. (**Figure 6-16**)

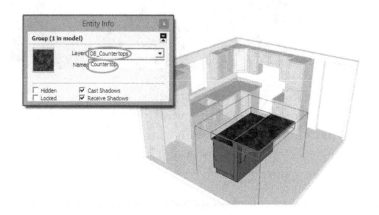

Do the same thing for the exterior cabinets by entering that group, creating the countertop objects and grouping them together into their own object layer group also named **Countertops**. Assign them to the layer **OB_Countertops**. (**Figure 6-17**)

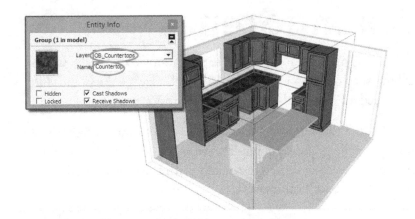

Figure 6-17
Separate each
countertop
part into its
own group.
Then group
the assembly
together.

Adding Details

At this point you should understand the basic organizational structure of the model. You divided your model into major locations (Island and Exterior), then you grouped similar objects together within each of them. This makes it easier to assign objects to layers because you don't have to manually assign each object to a specific layer, you just need to make sure it is placed within the correct group.

Continue going through the model and add appliances, plumbing, window, doors, etc, creating your own object layer groups as necessary in order to maintain a well organized model. (**Figure 6-18**)

Figure 6-18
Add appliances,
trim, plumbing,
windows and
other details
to finish your
model.

Creating Scenes

In this model, I need to create elevation views of each wall of cabinets, as well as a front, side, and back view of the island. I'll also need an overall plan view from the top.

Because the primary purpose of the model was to create a highly detailed rendering model, I've made it a little harder for me to dimension the cabinets, especially with the crown molding at the top of the wall cabinets.

To help overcome this, I will create a special scene that hides certain object layers and renders a simple style that I can toggle to just when doing dimensions in LayOut.

Styles

For this project, there are a few different styles I used for modeling, and for setting up the various scenes:

✓ **Modeling** - This is my default modeling style. It has simple, straight edges and fully textured materials. It hides all section plane objects and active cuts by default. This is the style that is active 90% of the time during the process of creating a model.

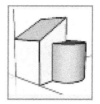

✓ **Elevations** - This is the style I save with elevation scenes. It's a somewhat sketchy style, but is fully colored and textured. The Background is white. It hides all section plane objects and guides but keeps active cuts visible.

✓ **Dimensioning** - This is a special style I use to create a scene that I can temporarily switch to while dimensioning in LayOut. It's a style with straight lines, shaded materials (no textures),

and it also hides section planes but keeps active section cuts. Also note that it shows guides in case you've placed some to help you snap dimensions to.

Utility Scene

In this kitchen model, there is crown molding that goes along the top of the cabinets. In LayOut, I actually want to snap dimensions to the top corners of the cabinets, but the molding covers those points.

To get around this, I created a utility scene that allows me to hide the moldings temporarily without changing the camera perspective of the scene. You can create this scene by hiding unnecessary layers such as appliances and moldings, setting the style to something simple, and saving the scene. (**Figure 6-19**)

U_Dimensioning Scene

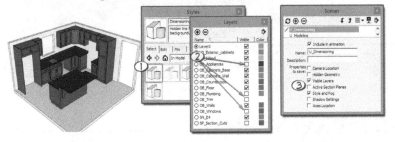

Figure 6-19
Create a utility scene that only saves layer visibility and style.

1. Select a simple style with solid material colors and straight lines to make it easy to snap dimensions to.

2. Hide all objects you don't need to snap dimensions to. (In this case, I hid the trim layer and the appliances.)

3. Create a new scene that only remembers visible layers and style.

The key is to make sure the **Camera Location** property of the scene is unchecked. This will let you switch back and forth between elevation scenes and this utility scene without moving the model in the viewport.

Perspective Scene

The cover page of the construction drawings is a great place to put a perspective view of the entire model. (**Figure 6-20**)

To do this, simply make all layers visible, set the camera to a perspective you like, select a style and save the scene with all properties saved. Save this scene as **V1_Perspective**.

Figure 6-20
A perspective scene is great for the cover page of your construction documents.

Plan View Scenes

For the plan view, I want to see the base cabinets, wall cabinets, countertops and appliances all from the same perspective. The problem is that from a top view, the countertop completely hides the base cabinets from view.

In order to get the look I want, I'm going to create two different scenes so I can create separate viewports for the base cabinets and the wall cabinets. For a detailed step by step on how to do this, see the chapter titled "Stacking Viewports."

V2_Basecabs

1. To set my **visible objects,** I want to hide the wall cabinets, crown molding, and window.

2. I don't have to worry about **foreground depth or background depth** since I am not creating a section cut through anything and there's nothing in the background that needs to be hidden.

3. I'll set the **camera perspective** to parallel projection mode and orient it in top view, looking down from above.

4. For the **style**, I will be using X-ray mode to see through the countertop in order to see the base cabinets underneath. I need to make sure I have the floor object hidden, or else the faces from the floor will cause a discoloration in the viewport.

   Save the scene as **V2_Basecabs**. The result is a top view of the kitchen with the base cabinets and countertops both visible because of the Xray style. (**Figure 6-21**)

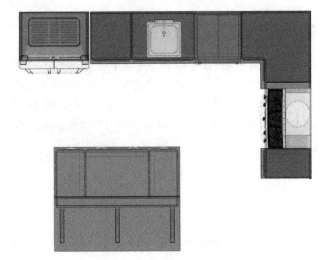

Figure 6-21
This scene saves an X-ray style so the cabinets and countertops are both visible.

V2_Wallcabs

For the next scene, I'll invert the layers so only the wall cabinets and crown moldings are visible. I don't want to change the camera perspective, since this will be placed directly over the base cabinet viewport in LayOut. (**Figure 6-22**)

I'll change the style so it's not in Xray mode. I'll use a basic solid textured style for this scene. Save this in a scene labeled **V2_Wallcabs**.

Figure 6-22
This scene will be overlaid on top of the base cabinet viewport in LayOut.

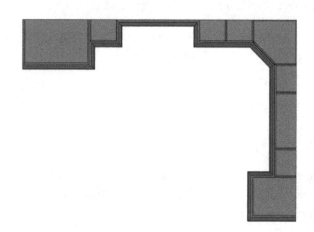

Elevation Scenes

I like using full color drawings for kitchens in order to highlight the overall look of the cabinets, close to what they'll look like in real life. In order to create the proper elevation view I need, I'll also have to create a section cut through the adjacent cabinetry.

I will use the **SectionCutFace** plugin to create linework and apply a hatch pattern to.

V3_Sink

The first elevation scene we'll create will be facing the sink.

1. **Visible Objects** - We can define our visible objects by activating all of the layers except the island. (Even though the island will most likely be hidden behind our section plane, it's

still good practice to hide layers you know don't need to be visible in a scene.)

2. **Foreground Depth** - Insert a new section plane object and place it at a location where you cut an outline of a wall cabinet and a base cabinet. You want to try to avoid any appliances. Don't forget, you can lock the orientation of a section plane by holding the **SHIFT** key. I found a good spot about 6" away from the corner of the countertop. (**Figure 6-23**)

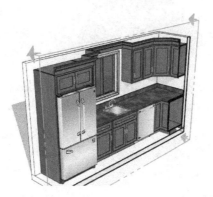

Figure 6-23
Insert a section cut object to define your foreground depth.

3. **Background Depth** - We don't need to worry about background depth in this case. (There's nothing in the background we need to hide.)

4. **Camera Perspective** - Right-click on the section plane and select "align view" to set our camera perspective. Make sure we've gone to **Camera -> Parallel projection**, and zoom in to get the camera aligned properly. (**Figure 6-24**)

5. **Style** - I like showing some shadows in my elevations, so enable shadows and adjust the sliders until you've created a shadow that you like. I tend to lighten up the shadow quite a bit in order to avoid any confusion from anyone looking at the drawings.

Figure 6-24
Align the
camera and set
the style you'd
like to save in
the scene.

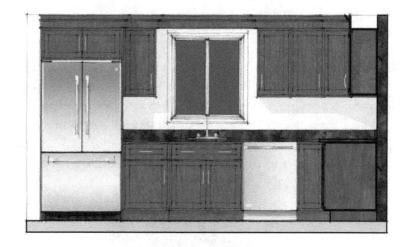

Activate the style you'd like to save with the scene. In this case I created a style with full textures and sketchy lines.

Figure 6-25
Save all the
scene properties
for the V3_Sink
scene.

Save the scene with all the properties saved. (**Figure 6-25**) We'll come back later to create the linework we will be using for the section cut hatching. For now, we'll leave this as is.

V4_Oven

To create the next elevation we'll switch back to the Modeling scene to quickly disable any active section cuts and to reset our layer visibility states.

Follow the same procedure for the next elevation, defining the visible objects, foreground depth, background depth, camera perspective, and style.

1. Set **visible objects** by activating all layers except the island.

2. Set **foreground depth** by creating a section cut through the adjacent cabinetry.

3. If needed, define your **background depth**. (In this case, we don't need to.)

4. Align the **camera** to the section plane object, and set the camera to parallel perspective.

5. Customize the **style** by setting shadows and choosing a preset style from the **Styles window**.

Save a new scene, saving all scene properties. Name the scene **V4_Oven**. Don't worry about the parts of the model that have been cut open by the section cut, you'll take care of that later. For now, let's continue setting up the preliminary scenes. (**Figure 6-26**)

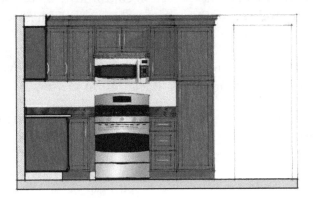

Figure 6-26
Oven elevation scene.

V5_Island, V5_Island_Left, V5_Island_Back

For the island elevations, you'll find it very easy to configure since we took the time to separate the exterior cabinets from the island cabinets.

Create scenes for the front, side and back of the island as follows:

1. Set **Visible Objects** by hiding **LO_Exterior_Cabinets, OB_Floor, OB_Walls, OB_Windows**, and **SP_Section_Cuts**. (**Figure 6-27**)

Figure 6-27
Isolate the island by hiding layers that you don't want to see.

2. We don't need to create a section cut through anything, so our **Foreground Depth** will be defined simply by where we place the camera.

3. With all other layers hidden except for the island, we've also taken care of having to set a **Background Depth**.

4. For these elevations you can **orient your camera** using many different methods. Try using the **Position Camera tool**, or try using some of the preset camera positions in SketchUp.

5. Set your **Style** and your shadow settings.

Save the scenes with all properties saved. Make sure to label the scenes so it is easier to recall them when in LayOut. (**Figure 6-28**)

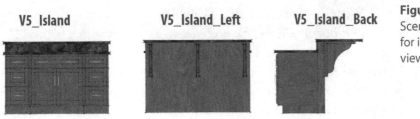

V5_Island   **V5_Island_Left**   **V5_Island_Back**

Figure 6-28
Scenes saved
for island
viewports.

Export to LayOut

With the scenes saved in SketchUp, the creation of the LayOut document will be pretty easy. Start out with a blank 11" x 17" template file in LayOut. Insert your viewports, then add annotations and dimensions. For step by step instructions on how to do these things in LayOut, see the part of this book named LayOut Documents.

Dimensions

In this model, the crown molding covers up the top of the wall cabinets when in elevation view. This would make it hard to snap dimensions to, but we created a special scene just for this situation.

The **Dimensions** scene only saves layer visibility and style, so we can use it to help us when we need to add dimensions to these wall cabinets. (**Figure 6-29**)

1. Insert your viewport as you normally would, assigning it to the appropriate scene to orient the camera and scale it to the proper size.

2. When you are ready to start inserting dimensions, temporarily switch to the **Dimensions** scene. The camera perspective won't change, but the crown molding will disappear, letting you snap dimensions to the cabinets.

Figure 6-29 The Dimensions scene hides the crown molding and lets you snap dimensions to the cabinets.

3. When you're done dimensioning, change the viewport back to the original scene.

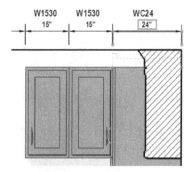

Cover Page

On the cover page, insert a viewport on the model layer and set the scene to **V1_Perspective**. Resize it to fill the page. Then, switch to the annotation layer and insert an elevation marker from the scrapbook and change the text. (**Figure 6-30**)

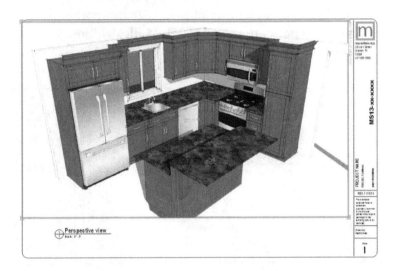

Cover Page Layer Organization

Layer	Contents	Scale
Dimensions	Elevation marker	N/A
Models2	-	-
Models	**V1_Perspective**	Perspective
TitleBlock	Titleblock elements	N/A

Plan View

The plan view is going to be constructed from two viewports by stacking them on top of each other. For step by step instructions on how to stack viewports, see the section named Stacking Viewports.

Insert the first viewport onto the **Models** layer and set the scene to **V2_Basecabs**. Copy and paste that viewport onto the **Models2** layer and set the scene to **V3_Wallcabs**. Both viewports should be set to a scale of 3/4" = 1'0". (**Figure 6-31**)

Figure 6-31
Kitchen plan view page.

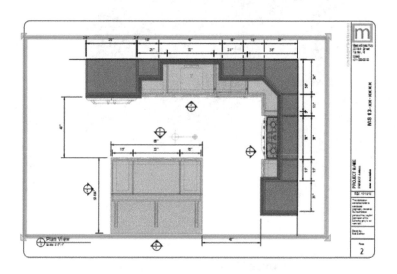

Plan View Layer Organization

Layer	Contents	Scale
Dimensions	Dimensions, Annotations	3/4" = 1'-0"
Models2	**V2_Wallcabs**	3/4" = 1'-0"
Models	**V2_Basecabs**	3/4" = 1'-0"
TitleBlock	Titleblock elements	N/A

Sink Elevation

The sink elevation will have some section cut linework that we'll create and import onto this page. We'll use the **SectionCutFace** plugin to create a group from the section cut, then we'll simply copy and paste it into LayOut. (**Figure 6-32**)

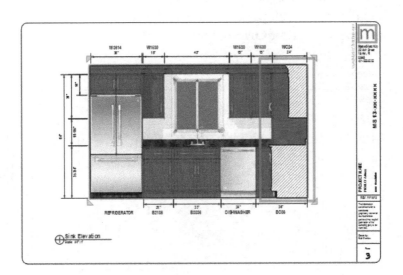

Figure 6-32
Kitchen Sink
elevation page.

Sink Elevation Layer Organization

Layer	Contents	Scale
Dimensions	Dimensions, Annotations	3/4" = 1'-0"
Models2	**Pasted Linework**	3/4" = 1'-0"
Models	**V3_Sink**	3/4" = 1'-0"
TitleBlock	Titleblock elements	N/A

Oven Elevation

The oven elevation will share the same process as the last page, in that we'll create section cut linework to stack on top of the main viewport.

Remember that you can add a material to linework faces in SketchUp before you paste it into LayOut, or you can right-click the **viewport -> Edit Original** to edit it after it's imported. (**Figure 6-33**)

Figure 6-33
Kitchen Oven
elevation page.

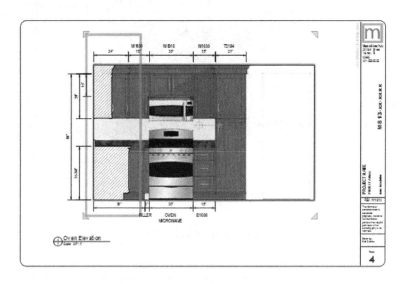

Oven Elevation Layer Organization

Layer	Contents	Scale
Dimensions	Dimensions, Annotations	3/4" = 1'-0"
Models2	**Pasted Linework**	3/4" = 1'-0"
Models	**V4_Oven**	3/4" = 1'-0"
TitleBlock	Titleblock elements	N/A

Island Elevations

On the last page we will insert three viewports of the front, back and side of the island. Since they are not overlapping each other they can all be placed on the same layer. (**Figure 6-34**)

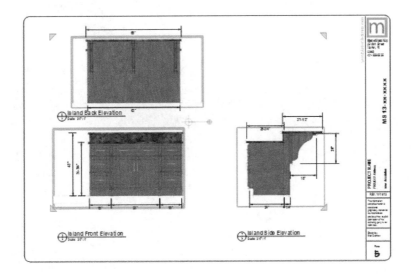

Figure 6-34
Kitchen Island elevation page.

Island Elevations Layer Organization

Layer	Contents	Scale
Dimensions	Dimensions, Annotations	3/4" = 1'-0"
Models2	-	-
Models	**V5_Island, V5_Island_left, V5_Island_back**	3/4" = 1'-0"
TitleBlock	Titleblock elements	N/A

Project Overview

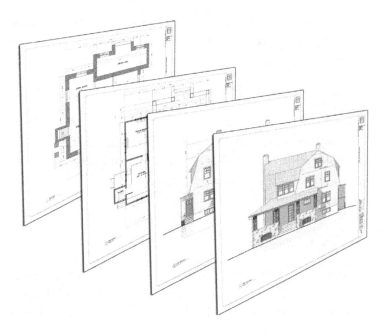

Figure 7-1
Sample pages
from the House
project file in
LayOut.

This is a project that consists of floor plans and exterior elevations of a house. In this project, you'll learn the following:

✓ Organize your model layers so you can isolate visibility by floor, and object type.

✓ Create two versions of certain objects, each optimized for either 2D plan views, or 3D rendered views.

✓ Use section planes to create views of your model to bring into LayOut.

✓ Use multiple section planes in complex models in order to create the view you want.

✓ Disguise edges that you don't want to be seen in your model.

✓ Use dynamic components to save modeling time for objects like doors and windows.

✓ Create multiple scenes from the same perspective in order to overlay viewports in LayOut for more control over the way your model looks.

✓ Apply hatching to your model using various methods. Model Setup.

To follow along with this project, open up the file **Farmhouse.skp**. (**Figure 7-1**) That is the completed model where you can dig in and see exactly how the model is organized and set up for LayOut.

Project Goals

Before starting the project, I had to assess what the purpose of the model was. By thinking about this ahead of time I can make decisions about the level of detail I want to incorporate into my model before I start modeling.

The primary purpose of the model is to create floor plans that I can bring into LayOut. So I am going to make a **coordination model**. This means that I need to focus on building simple, with relatively low levels of detail that has well defined points for snapping dimensions to.

The secondary purpose is to create a **rendering model**. I am not going to create a photorealistic render, but I would like to produce some 3D perspective images from the model to use in my presentation. This means I may need to build some parts of the house in higher detail in order to create the desired effect.

I know I am only creating one master model, so I'll need to make some special considerations in order to build both a **coordination model** and a **rendering model** all within the same file.

You would usually start modeling for a little bit to get some of the basic structure created before pausing to start creating the initial organizational groups, but I want to go over the basic organization of the model first before we start creating anything.

Phase/Location Layer Groups

The overall structure of the model starts by organizing the model into different **phase/location layer groups**, then grouping objects within those sections into **object layer groups**. (**Figure 7-2**) If a project is split into multiple phases, or if it's a remodel and you have existing conditions, demolition, and new construction, your first set of organization would exist between these scopes of work.

In this case, I don't have any phased work, so I'm only splitting the project up by physical location. Splitting your model into physical sections serves two purposes:

1. It makes it easier to model because you can isolate your workspace and **Outliner window** to only show you the area of work you are currently working on. (It is hard to place objects inside the first floor when it is covered up by the second floor. By separating them, you can hide the second floor in order to expose the first.)

2. It separates your model into logical sections that correspond directly to viewports you want to create in LayOut. If you know there is a specific viewport you need to create, you need to organize your model in a way that lets you easily isolate those objects from the rest of your model.

Figure 7-2
Create groups
for each floor of
the house and
assign them to
their own layers.

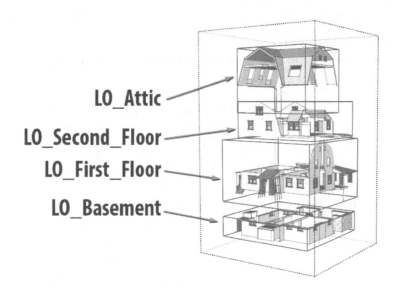

LO_Attic

LO_Second_Floor

LO_First_Floor

LO_Basement

This house has a basement, 1st, 2nd, and 3rd floor, so I have
created a layer for each, and a special group for each of those layers.

✓ Basement group - Assigned to layer **LO_Basement**

✓ 1st Floor group - Assigned to layer **LO_First Floor**

✓ 2nd Floor group - Assigned to layer **LO_Second Floor**

✓ 3rd Floor group - Assigned to layer **LO_Third Floor**

By splitting up my model this way, I am forced to divide my
exterior walls into sections that correspond to the proper layer.
Sometimes this can be counter intuitive. For instance, my gable
walls span from the first floor all the way to the third floor. In
order to isolate the sections of the house by floor, I have to split
up the gable walls into different sections and place them on the
appropriate layer group.

Sometimes it makes sense to do this, other times it doesn't.
With a gambrel style house like this, it is much easier to draw the
gable walls as one continuous wall, as opposed to drawing one floor
at a time. **To show both ways of doing it, I drew one of the walls**

continuous so you can see how it affects the overall process of setting up scenes and bringing them into LayOut.

Object Layer Groups

Within each location specific group, are another set of layer groups that hold all similar items. (**Figure 7-3**) These groups are all assigned to various **object layers**. Here are some examples of object layer groups you'll find within the location groups;

- ✓ **OB_Chimneys**

- ✓ **OB_Floors**

- ✓ **OB_Furniture**

- ✓ **OB_Gutters**

- ✓ **OB_Roof**

- ✓ **OB_Stairs**

- ✓ **OB_Structural**

- ✓ **OB_Walls_Exterior**

- ✓ **OB_Walls_Interior**

- ✓ **OB_Windows/Doors**

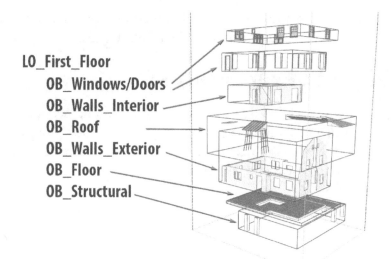

Figure 7-3
Within each
location layer
group, assign
similar objects
to their object
layer group.

LO_First_Floor
  OB_Windows/Doors
  OB_Walls_Interior
  OB_Roof
  OB_Walls_Exterior
  OB_Floor
  OB_Structural

Inside each of those groups you'll find all the objects that should be assigned to that object layer. Here's an example. If you select a window that's located on the first floor, you'll find it is in the **Windows** group (assigned to the **OB_Windows/Doors** layer), inside of the **1st Floor** group (assigned to the **LO_First_Floor** layer). The window itself isn't assigned any layer other than the default **Layer0.** But you will be able to control its visibility because it inherits the layers of the other groups that it is in.

So if you hide the **OB_Windows/Doors** layer, that window will hide. Or, if you wanted to hide everything on the 1st floor, you could just hide the **LO_First_Floor** layer, and everything within any groups assigned to that layer, (like the window), will hide.

Confused yet? Be sure to check it out yourself in SketchUp to better understand how the model is organized.

Special Layers

There are a few special layers in this model that you'll notice. I had to create these special layers because I was creating one model for two different purposes. The primary purpose of my model is to create coordination drawings, but I also wanted to use the same model to create renderings.

In my model I used a special dynamic component door model that would allow me to show an open door with a dashed door swing arc in plan view, but to show a closed door in elevation or 3D perspective views. I created two different layers for each "state" of the door in order to be able to control that. (**Figure 7-4**)

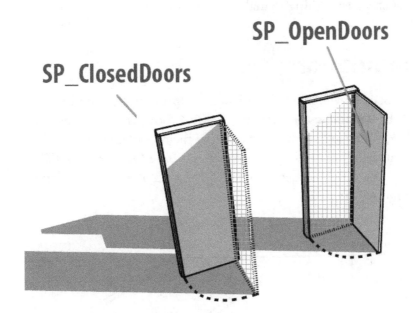

SP_OpenDoors

SP_ClosedDoors

Figure 7-4
Special layers for the doors let me toggle whether they appear open or closed.

TIPS These doors are included as a bonus with this book. By using the **Interact tool,** you can open or close the door. With the door closed, use the **Scale tool (S)** to resize the door to the opening. Toggle the two built-in layers depending upon whether you're in plan view or elevation view.

Start Modeling

My modeling process usually cycles between periods of drawing, and periods of organizing. You should always try to organize while you draw, but sometimes you need to just focus on modeling for a while. You can then take a break from drawing and just check everything to make sure its is in the proper group or layer.

Foundation

Start drawing your foundation footprint using a combination of the **Rectangle tool (R)** and the **Line tool (L)**. Feed accurate dimensions to SketchUp by entering them into your keyboard immediately after using a tool. Use the **Tape Measure tool (T)** to create guides as needed in order to help you draw the foundation. (**Figure 7-5**)

Figure 7-5
Use the **Tape Measure tool (T)** to create guides while you model the foundation footprint.

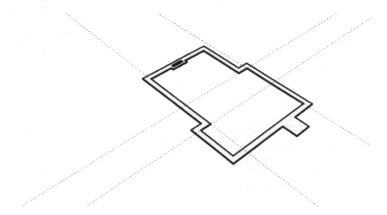

With the outline completed, use the **Offset tool (F)** to define the thickness of the foundation. Using the **Push/Pull tool (P)**, extrude to the height of your foundation walls. (If you need to show a wider footing, extrude to the thickness of your footing, then use the **Offset tool (F)** to create the outline of the walls, then extrude to the wall height.)

I like to isolate entities into groups immediately after extruding them, if not sooner. Go ahead and triple-click the foundation walls to select all of it, right-click, select "Make Group". (**Figure 7-6**) We'll do a little more drawing before we start assigning groups to layers.

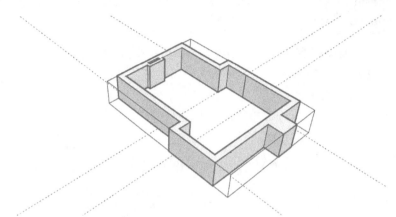

Figure 7-6
Extrude the foundation and make it into a group.

First Floor

Let's continue by building the first floor exterior shell so we can start to see our model take shape. We will need to draw the floor and the exterior walls next.

TIP Are you going to draw each floor joist, wall sheathing, siding, subfloor, etc? You need to ask yourself this before you start modeling. Refer back to the goals you created for your model before you started. In this case, I am only creating an overall floor plan model, so drawing each joist would be extra unnecessary work. I am simply going to draw an outline of the space that **represents** the floor assembly.

Even if you plan on creating a framing plan from your model, I'd recommend first starting out with a representation of the floor structure before drawing each framing member until you have come closer to the final design of the model. You can always go back and add details later. It's much easier to make changes to basic shapes in your model than to have to edit a bunch of joist components.

Since the floor and walls are going to share the same perimeter footprint of the foundation walls, we can copy and paste some of the entities from the foundation in order to help us get started with the first floor.

To copy entities from one group and paste them into another, follow these steps: (Figure 7-7)

Figure 7-7
Copy and paste entities from the foundation group to help create the first floor.

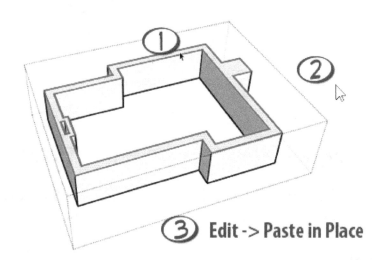

③ Edit -> Paste in Place

Step by Step

1. Open up the foundation group and select the top face. Hit **CTRL + C (Command + C on Mac)** on your keyboard to copy it.

2. Click outside the foundation group to close it.

3. Go to **Edit -> Paste In Place**.

This will paste the entities you had copied in the same physical location that they were located, only they will reside on whichever group you are currently in.

Since you aren't in any group right now, they will simply paste into your main model.

TIP Using Paste In Place is a great way to move objects from one group to another group without moving their physical location. This is great when you realize you've accidentally assigned an object to the wrong layer group, and would like to move it to a different one. I highly recommend creating a custom keyboard shortcut so you can quickly copy and paste objects to different groups. I use **SHIFT + V**.

With the outline of the foundation pasted, we need to heal the face in the center of the space in order to start building our floor object. Simply retrace over one of the inner edges and a face will appear.

At this time, triple-click the new face and create a new group. Enter the group by double-clicking it with the **Select tool (Spacebar)** to finish creating the 1st floor. (**Figure 7-8**)

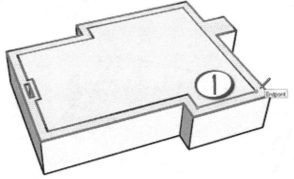

Figure 7-8
Trace over one of the interior lines with the **Line tool (L)** to fill in a face. Then, isolate everything into a new group.

TIP Another keyboard shortcut I use all the time activates **View -> Component Edit -> Hide Rest of Model**. I've assigned this to the letter X. I use this ALL THE TIME. It's a quick way to hide other objects in your model while you are working within a group. I find it to be essential in order to model without losing my mind.

Inside the floor group, double-click the new face you just created so the inner edges become highlighted. Tap Delete to get rid of them. (**Figure 7-9**) You should be left with one solid surface in the outline of the foundation walls. Use the **Push/Pull tool (P)** to extrude the floor to the height you need. (**Figure 7-10**)

Figure 7-9
Enter the floor group and double-click the inner face and delete it.

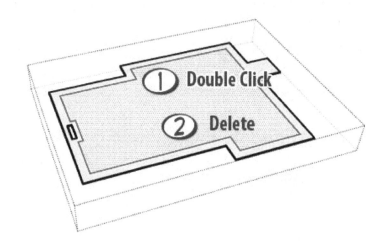

Figure 7-10
Use the push/ pull tool to extrude the floor.

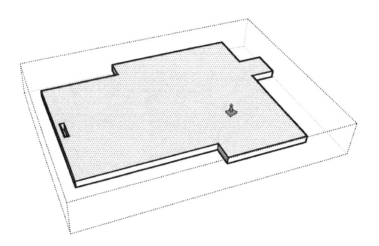

Exterior Walls

Next we'll create the first floor exterior walls, so we'll use the same technique to copy and paste an outline from the floor edges to help us start drawings our walls. Enter the floor group by double-clicking on it, select the face, press **CTRL + C (Command + C on Mac)** to copy. Exit the floor group, then go to **Edit -> paste in place**. (**Figure 7-11**) Use the **Offset tool (F)** to define the thickness of your walls, delete the face in the center, extrude to the height of your walls. Triple-click the walls and make into a group.

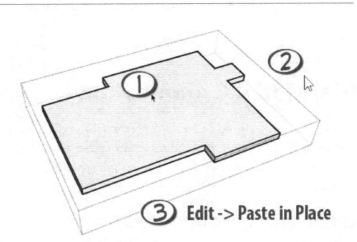

Figure 7-11
Copy the floor surface, exit the group, then paste in place.

Again, with the walls we are not drawing every stud, sheet of plywood or drywall. We are just creating a simple outline that is **representative** of the wall assembly.

Continue modeling like this until you have drawn all of the floors/ceilings, and exterior walls for each floor. (**Figure 7-12**)

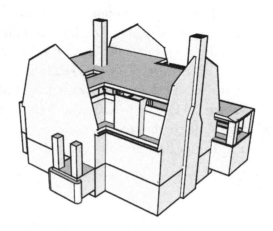

Figure 7-12
All the exterior
walls and floors
are modeled.

Initial Model Organization

At this point, I would pause and review all the different parts you've created and assign them to their associated phase/location layer in order to help you visualize the overall structure of your model.

Location Layer Groups

Select the first floor wall group and the first floor group and make a new group with them. Assign this group to the layer **LO_ First_Floor** by going to the **Entity Info window** while the group is selected and selecting the appropriate layer from the drop down menu.

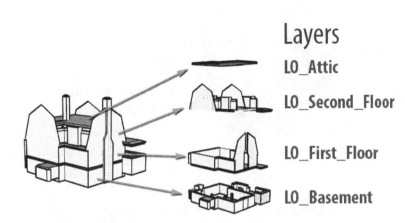

Figure 7-13
Select the floors
and walls and
group them by
level. Assign
those groups to
a unique layer.

Do the same for **LO_Second_Floor** and **LO_Attic** by selecting the wall and floor group, making a new group then assigning it to the appropriate layer. We will do the same thing for the basement (**LO_Basement**) eventually, but since there is only one object (the foundation wall group) we'll leave it as is for now.

You should now have your model organized by location (**Figure 7-13**)

Object Layer Groups

Within each level of the house, you'll now want to assign each object to their appropriate object layers. Since you've got the model split up by floor, you can hide the rest of the model while you work on each floor of the house. This makes it much easier to model.

Go through each floor of the house, and group all similar types of objects together into a master object layer group, and assign that master group to the appropriate layer. (**Figure 7-14, Figure 7-15**)

Figure 7-14
Within the first floor group, select all the floor objects and assign them to the **OB_ Floors** layer.

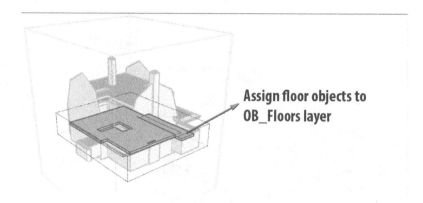

Assign floor objects to
OB_Floors layer

Figure 7-15
Within the first floor group, select all the exterior wall objects and assign them to the **OB_Walls_ exterior** layer.

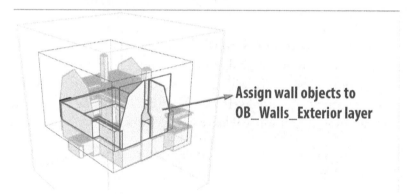

Assign wall objects to
OB_Walls_Exterior layer

Create Utility Scenes

As you start building more of the details in your model, you'll find it really helpful to set up some basic scenes, one for each floor of the house. Isolate one level of the house by hiding the other layers, make sure your preferred modeling style is active and save a new scene. Do this for each floor. (**Figure 7-16**)

Now, as you model, you will quickly be able to focus in on one area of your model at a time without having to manually change layers and styles each time: A huge time saver.

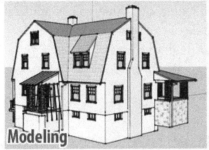
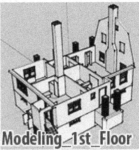
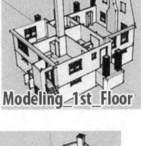
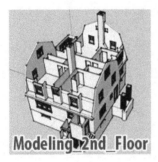

Utility Scenes

Modeling

Modeling_1st_Floor

Modeling_2nd_Floor

Modeling_Attic

Figure 7-16
Create scenes
for each floor
that hide certain
layers that
would obstruct
your view while
modeling.

Interior Walls

Hide all levels but the **LO_First_Floor** layer. Open the first floor group. Start drawing your interior walls using the **Rectangle tool (R), Line tool (L),** and **Tape Measure tool (T)**. I prefer adding my door openings after I've extruded the walls, but there are plenty of people who like to locate them before extruding them. (**Figure 7-17**)

You can draw the entire outline of all the walls in 2D first, then extrude them all at once, or you can extrude one wall, then continue to build off of it in 3D. It's up to you. I prefer creating all of my interior walls as separate groups as I find it easier to manipulate and resize them. Then, once I've finalized the layout I'll typically explode them into one group.

Regardless of the way you do it, you'll want to have at least one group deemed the "object layer group" that you assign to the layer **OB_Walls_Interior.** Inside of that group you may have multiple unnamed groups of different walls, or you may just have ungrouped entities that make up all of your interior walls together. The choice is yours.

Figure 7-17
Within the first floor group, draw the interior walls for that floor.

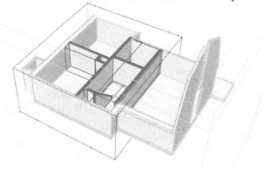

Interior walls within the LO_First_Floor Layer Group

Continue drawing walls for each level of the house, making sure you are inside of the correct group each time you start drawing. It becomes really easy when you keep the **Outliner window** open. (**Figure 7-18**)

Figure 7-18
The **Outliner window** is a great way to navigate your model while modeling.

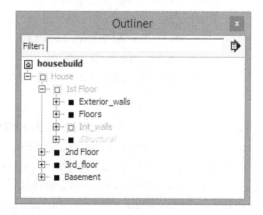

For instance, when you are ready to start drawing the second story interior walls, go to the **Outliner window**, and expand the second floor group, and double-click on the interior walls group and start drawing. (If there is no interior walls group yet, you'll need to create one. But this is a great way to make sure you're not duplicating any layer groups either.)

Doors/Windows

Creating doors and windows requires two steps. First, you need to cut the opening of the window in the wall where you want the window to be. Then you need to insert and resize the window to fit the opening.

TIP - Some components can be made to "self-cut" a wall so you don't have to go through this two step process. For now, I'll assume you are either building your window and door components yourself or are using components that do not have this feature.

First you'll need to go through your entire model and create openings for each window and door in the house. I will typically size the openings to the nominal dimensions. You may want to size them to the actual rough opening dimensions. Just keep in mind, you need to be able to snap dimensions to something in LayOut, so think of what dimension you want shown on your drawings.

To create a wall opening, open the wall group that you want to edit. Use the **Rectangle Tool (R)** to draw an opening to the size you need. Use the **Tape Measure tool (T)** and **Move tool (M)** to reposition and resize if needed. Use the **Push/Pull tool (P)** to punch a hole in the wall by referencing a point or edge in plane with the back of the wall. **(Figure 7-19)** Continue to do this until all of the door and window openings are created.

Figure 7-19 Use the **Tape Measure tool (T)** to place guides, then use the **Rectangle Tool (R)** to draw door and window openings. Push/ pull them to delete the surface.

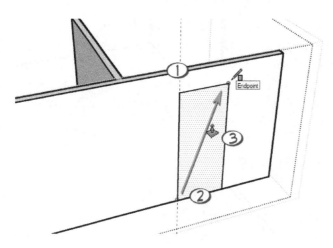

For the process of inserting doors and windows, I highly recommend using pre-made dynamic components. Dynamic components have many features including the ability to constrain proportions. This allows you to quickly scale a component's overall size without affecting the proportions of things such as moldings, mullions, jamb thickness, etc.

Using dynamic components, you can quickly go through your model inserting windows and doors into the openings you created in your walls and resize them to fit. (**Figure 7-20**)

Figure 7-20 Once a door opening is created, insert dynamic components that can be resized to the opening.

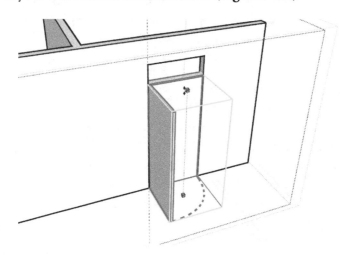

Organizing Doors/Windows

As with everything you create in SketchUp, you must think about how is it directly going to fit into the workflow of bringing your model into LayOut. How much detail do you need to show, and what details should you be leaving out?

In my house model, I used window components downloaded from the 3D warehouse modeled by the SketchUp team. They were great because they allowed me to scale the windows to size without having to manually resize the mullions or the jambs. I did have to manually add the casings to the exterior of the windows, which added a significant amount of time to the modeling process.

The windows were perfect because they looked great for both purposes of creating coordination drawings and creating a render from a 3D perspective. (**Figure 7-21**)

Figure 7-21
These dynamic windows from SketchUp let you resize them with the **Scale Tool (S)** without stretching the frames or mullions.

For the doors, I wanted them to provide some more functionality. I wanted to show a very simple door in a 90° open position when saving plan view scenes, and I wanted to show a dashed door swing arc so I wouldn't have to draw that in LayOut.

But when creating elevations or 3D perspective views, I wanted the doors to be in a closed position, and I wanted them to look a little more detailed as well. I decided to create two special layers, one for "Open Doors", and one for "Closed Doors". This allows me to control which version of the door I want to see when I'm saving a scene. (**Figure 7-22**)

Because of the dual requirements I needed from the door components, I created a custom dynamic door that could do both. The door is included with this book so feel free to use it in your projects.

Figure 7-22 These doors have two layer states that allow you to optimize the look of the door for plan view or for perspective views.

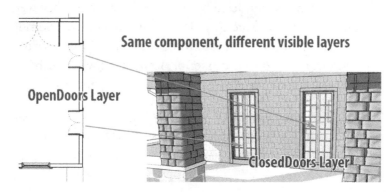

Roof

Even though you could say the main roof extends from the 3rd level down to the 2nd level, I decided not to split up the roof into each level. I found it much easier to model the roof as one object because, being a gambrel roof, it had multiple angles in it. (**Figure 7-23**)

Figure 7-23 The gambrel style roof with openings for the dormers.

To create the roof, I created a profile of one half of the roof, then created lines along the edges of the walls where the roof needed to go. Using the **Follow Me tool**, I extruded the roof profile along multiple paths to create the roof. (**Figure 7-24**)

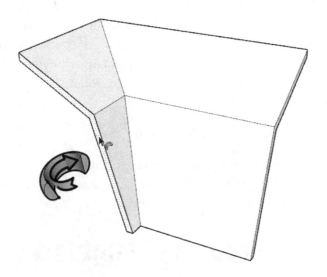

Figure 7-24
The **Follow Me tool** made it very easy to create the gambrel roof.

I placed the roof inside the **3rd_floor** group (which is assigned to the phase/location layer **LO_Attic**), inside an object group called **roof** (which is assigned to the object layer **OB_Roof**.) Inside that group I had the main roof, as well as individual groups for each dormer. All of those sub-groups remain on the default **Layer0**.

The roof for the front and back porch both reside on the **1st Floor** group (which is assigned to the **phase/location** layer **LO_First_Floor**), inside an object group called **roof,** (which is assigned to the object layer **OB_Roof**)

Materials

At this point you might feel it's a good time to start adding some textures to your model. I like to use simple black & white textures when creating coordination drawings to save on ink and to make less distractions from the dimensions and annotations.

If you're creating a photorealistic model, you'll want to use high quality colorful materials on your model. You may also just prefer the look of full colored drawings, the choice is yours.

If you purchased the Professional package along with this book, you'll have access to over 70 different black & white CAD style hatch materials that I use in my construction drawings. If you didn't purchase the Professional package, you can buy them separately at the link below.

www.SketchUptoLayOut.com/bonuspacks

Sometimes, when you paint materials in your model, you want to make sure you are painting the actual surface entity, and not just overriding the default material of a group.

Figure 7-25
Painting a group is different from painting a face directly.

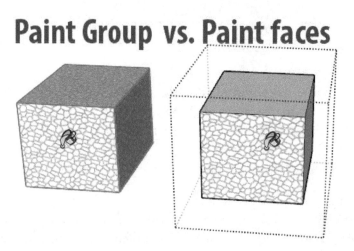

Paint Group vs. Paint faces

For example, if you apply the paint bucket tool to a group, all of the faces in that group that have the default material will inherit the new material you applied to the group. But if you open the group, you can apply materials to each individual face inside the group. (**Figure 7-25**)

The reason you'd want to do this is first of all you might need to apply different materials to different faces in a group. But you may also have a situation where you need to align the orientation of a material across multiple faces.

Since the floors extend to the outside of the walls, it creates an ugly line and the faces are divided there within different groups. The reason this happens is because we decided to draw the floor as a basic extruded shape. In reality if we drew it more accurate to reality, the siding and sheathing of the house would extend over the floors and we wouldn't see that line. But we wanted to save time by modeling it a little less detailed than that.

So we'll have to do a few extra procedures in order to disguise that line and make it look like it's a continuous wall. First, we need to open each group and paint the walls and exposed floors with a siding material.

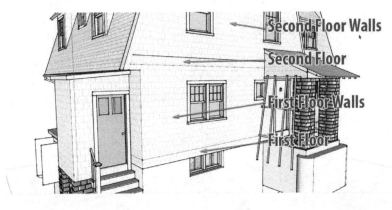

Figure 7-26
Paint the exterior of the walls and the exposed sides of the floors with the same material.

Open up the wall group and make sure you can select the individual entities in that group so you're sure you are painting an individual face. Select the material you want to use and paint that face. Then, without switching materials, go into the floor group and paint the exposed side of the floor. The materials should align. (**Figure 7-26**)

If they don't, you'll need to go back into one of the groups and sample the paint again by holding the **ALT key (Command key on**

Mac) and clicking on it with the paint bucket tool.

Once you've painted the faces, you might want to hide the edges that divide the various surfaces in order to create the illusion that it's one continuous wall. (**Figure 7-27**)

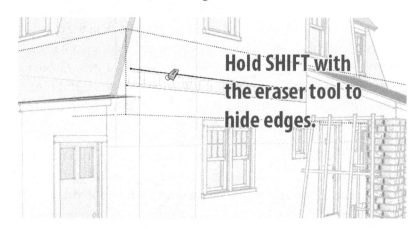

Hold SHIFT with the eraser tool to hide edges.

Adding Details

Go through the rest of the model and finish adding details. For instance, I didn't like the way the stone columns looked so I decided to make two versions. In one version I modeled each stone in the column to create some more detail. I placed that version on a layer called **SP_3D_Details**. (**Figure 7-28**)

Figure 7-28
Two versions of the stone columns on different layers give more control over the look of the model.

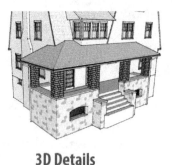

3D Details

2D Details

The original square version is much simpler, and I left it in the model because that is the version I will show for the plan views where I need clean points to snap to for dimensions. I put this version on a layer named **SP_2D_Details**. (**Figure 7-29**)

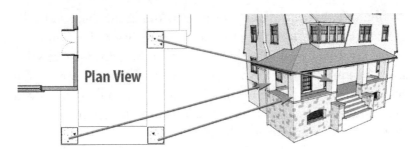

Figure 7-29
The simple square columns look great in plan view, but terrible in perspective view.

I also added gutters, chimney caps, hand rails, lattice work and more. You can always go back and add more detail as you model. It's good to get the main model built first before starting detail work though.

Creating Scenes

You've built the bulk of your model. You know there will still be changes, but you're ready to start bringing it into LayOut. If you've organized your model correctly, you shouldn't have to worry about making changes to your model after bringing it into LayOut. You can maintain a dynamic link between the two that allows you to instantly update your LayOut document to reflect any major changes made from the SketchUp model.

For this model, I am going to create plan views for each floor, and exterior elevations for each side of the house.

Styles

For this project, there are a few different styles I used for modeling, and for setting up the various scenes:

✓ **Modeling** - This is my default modeling style. It has simple, straight edges and fully textured materials. It hides all section plane objects and active cuts by default. This is the style that is active 90% of the time during the process of creating a model.

✓ **Plan Views** - This style is very simple, black and white. It has a white background to match the paper color in LayOut. It shows textures so you can see the material patterns.

✓ **Elevation Views** - Again, this is a pretty simple style, but it also includes a slightly stronger profile around the model.

Creating Plan Views

There are numerous ways to create plan views for LayOut. They can be simple, one scene viewports created by hiding various layers or they can be complex, made up of overlapping viewports and custom section cut linework. The level of complexity all depends upon the desired look and level of control you want to have over each viewport. We will look at a few different ways to create them.

For the basement, I wanted to apply a special concrete hatch pattern to the foundation walls, and I also wanted to have the ability to define a different line weight for the foundation walls when compared to everything else in scene.

To apply the hatching, use the **Parallel Perspective Hatching technique.** In order to control the lineweight independently, you'll need to create two separate scenes and overlay them as viewports once in LayOut. (**Figure 7-30**)

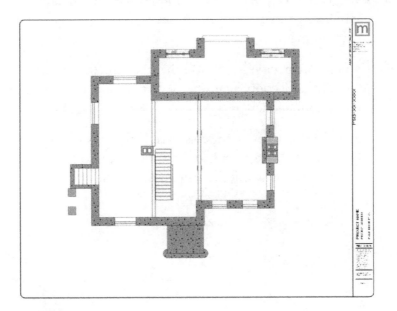

Figure 7-30
The foundation plan is made up of two stacked viewports.

P1_Basement

In this scene, you will want to only have the foundation walls visible. (**Figure 7-31**)

1. **Visible Objects** - Starting with all layers off, find the **phase/location layer** that the foundation walls are on. That would be the **LO_Basement** layer. Next, enable the appropriate object layer that the foundation walls are on.

   TIP In your SketchUp template, it's a good idea to create a scene that saves layer states where all layers are on, and another scene where all layers are off. This allows you to quickly hide or unhide layers to configure views.

2. **Foreground Depth** - Use the **Position Camera tool** to insert a clipping plane to expose the inside of the foundation walls. Select a point that slices through the windows so they show up in the scene.

3. **Background Depth** - You don't need to define a background depth because there's nothing in the background that you need to hide or mask.

4. **Camera Perspective** - Confirm that the camera perspective is in parallel projection, align the view, and zoom out enough to see the entire model.

5. **Style** - For plan view scenes, use a style that has simple, straight edges, a white background, and textured faces so the hatching and other materials will show up in the viewport.

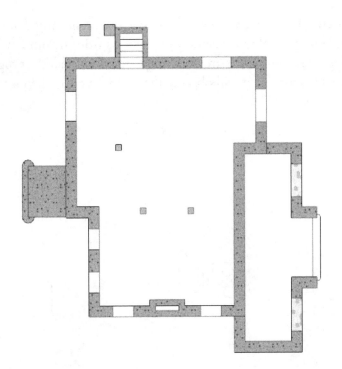

P1.2_Basement

For the second scene overlapping the foundation viewport, set the visible objects to show everything else in the basement except the foundation walls. (**Figure 7-32**)

1. **Visible Objects** - With the basement **phase/location layer** still active, hide the foundation wall object layer, and unhide all the other object layers in the model.

2. **Foreground Depth** - Not applicable; you're not making any section cuts.

3. **Background Depth** - Not applicable; There's nothing in the background you need to hide.

4. **Camera Perspective** - Choose the same camera settings as the previous scene so they will match when overlaid.

5. **Style** - Use the same style as the previous scene. You will be able to control line weight for viewports from within LayOut. Just make sure there are no background watermarks or fog enabled, or else it will obscure the first viewport when it is laid on top.

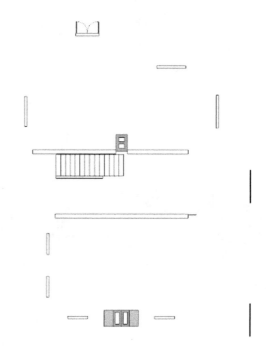

Figure 7-32
The basement windows, stairs, and chimneys are placed on a separate scene to have more control over their style

P2_FirstFloor, P2.2_FirstFloor

For the first floor, I want to show hatching for the walls and the chimneys. This time, we'll use the **SectionCutFace** plugin to quickly create filled linework.

Since I'm using a section cut through the walls, windows and doors in this scene, I'm going to stack another viewport on top of this one in LayOut with the stairs on it. Otherwise, if the stairs are visible in this first scene, they get sliced at a weird place and don't look right. (**Figure 7-33**)

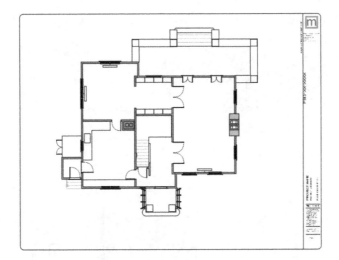

Figure 7-33
The first floor
is made up of
two viewports
and section cut
linework.

1. **Visible Objects** - Since we're going to be creating section cut linework, first unhide only the layers of objects you'd like linework created from. Hide everything except the first floor walls, stone columns, and chimneys. (Once the section cut linework is created, unhide any additional layers you'd like to see before saving the scene)

2. **Foreground Depth** - Create the section cut face using the **SectionCutFace** plugin, and paint the faces to the appropriate hatch material you'd like to use. Assign this linework to a layer created specifically for this scene because you don't want it to show up on any other scenes.

   TIP: If you're going to be inserting a lot of section planes, it may be a good idea to assign the section plane object to a scene specific layer as well. That way, your workspace doesn't clutter up too much when trying to insert more section planes later.

3. **Background Depth** - Not Applicable; You should be able to hide background objects by hiding their layers.

4. **Camera Perspective** - Confirm that the camera perspective is in parallel projection, align the view, and zoom out enough to see the entire model.

5. **Style** - Use the same style you created for the other plan view scenes.

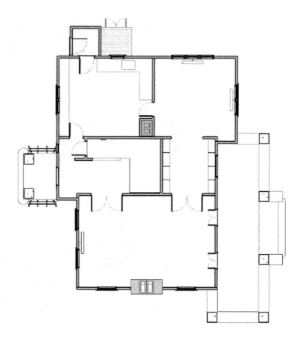

P3_SecondFloor

I'll use the same method I used in the first floor to create the scene for the second floor. One thing to note is that I wanted my **visible objects** to include the roof from the front and back porch, so I had to make sure the first floor master layer was active, and the roof object layer was also active.

P4_ThirdFloor

In this viewport, I wanted to show the total floorspace of the attic. This was challenging because of the compound angles created by the roof. (**Figure 7-35**)

First, for my visible objects, I included the first and second floor because I wanted their roof to show up in the background of the scene. I used the **SectionCutFace** plugin method again to create a slice of the model at floor level that I could paste into LayOut on top of the SketchUp viewport.

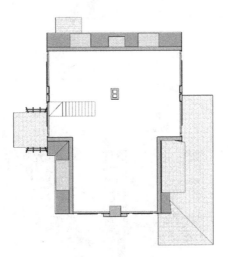

Figure 7-35
The roof had to be cut at floor level in order for the entire floor space to be visible.

Creating Elevations

The elevations were a little bit less complex because I did not need to create a section cut in any of them. I just turned on all the layers, and disabled the scene specific layers and the 2D detail layer, then oriented the camera for each perspective I wanted and created scenes for each.

However, in each scene I was concerned about the background depth. I wanted details that were showing in the background to appear lighter than the face of the wall I was looking at, so I used fog controls to do that.

Most of my time was spent tweaking various aspects of the style in order to achieve the look I was after. I prefer to have lighter colored materials in order to maintain a clean look on my drawings. You can do the same to materials in your model by sampling the material, going to the **Edit tab** in the **Materials**

window, and adjusting the slider.

I also enabled shadows in the elevation views. I made sure those weren't too dark either by adjusting the sliders in the **Shadows window**. (**Figure 7-36**)

Figure 7-36 In this elevation scene, you can see the fog adds to the depth of the scene.

Exporting to LayOut

Once you've created all the scenes, you can create a new LayOut project and begin importing your model into viewports on each page. Refer to the chapter on LayOut Documents for step by step instructions on importing SketchUp models, adding dimensions and annotations.

Basement Plan

On the cover page, insert a viewport on the **Model** layer and set the scene to **P1_basement**. Resize it to fill the page. Then, copy and paste the viewport onto the **Models2** layer and switch the scene to **P1.2_basement**. Switch to the annotation layer and insert an elevation marker from the scrapbook and change the text. (**Figure 7-37**)

Figure 7-37
Basement floor plan LayOut page.

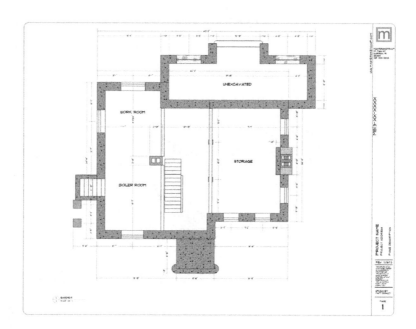

Basement Plan Layer Organization

Layer	Contents	Scale
Dimensions	Dimensions, Annotations	N/A
Models2	**P1.2_basement**	1/4" = 1'-0"
Models	**P1_basement**	1/4" = 1'-0"
TitleBlock	Titleblock elements	N/A

First Floor Plan

The first floor plan will be constructed from two regular viewports.

Insert a new viewport, set the scene to **P2_firstfloor** on the **Models** layer, then copy and paste it onto the **Models2** layer and set it to the **P2.2_firstfloor** scene.

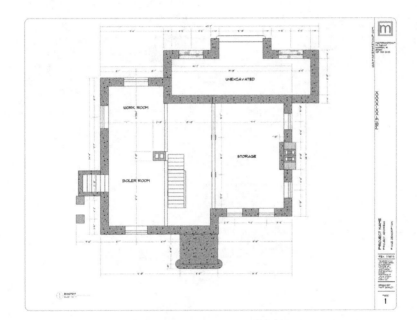

Figure 7-38
First floor plan
LayOut page

First Floor Plan Layer Organization

Layer	Contents	Scale
Dimensions	Dimensions, Annotations	N/A
Models2	**P2.2_firstfloor**	1/4" = 1'-0"
Models	**P2_firstfloor**	1/4" = 1'-0"
TitleBlock	Titleblock elements	N/A

Second Floor Plan

The second floor plan will be constructed from one viewport.

Insert a new viewport, set the scene to **P3_SecondFloor** on the **Models** layer.

Figure 7-39
Second floor
plan LayOut
page

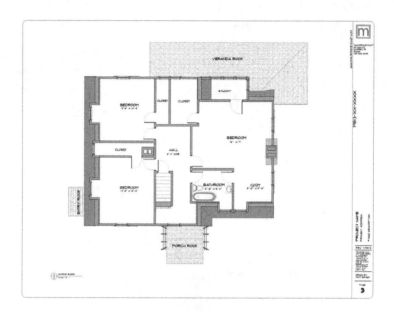

Second Floor Plan Layer Organization

Layer	Contents	Scale
Dimensions	Elevation marker	N/A
Models2	-	-
Models	**P3_SecondFloor**	1/4" = 1'-0"
TitleBlock	Titleblock elements	N/A

Attic Floor Plan

The attic floor plan will be constructed from one viewport.

Insert a new viewport, set the scene to **P4_ThirdFloor** on the **Models** layer.

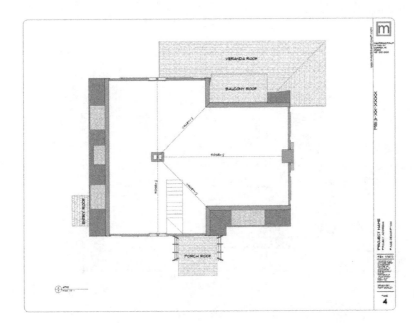

Figure 7-40
Attic floor plan
LayOut page.

Attic Floor Plan Layer Organization

Layer	Contents	Scale
Dimensions	Elevation marker	N/A
Models2	-	-
Models	**P4_ThirdFloor**	1/4" = 1'-0"
TitleBlock	Titleblock elements	N/A

Typical Elevations

The elevations are pretty much identical in how they are laid out. There is one viewport inserted next to the appropriate scene. Then, on the dimensions layer, I used the tools in LayOut to draw the ground level and I set a tonal pattern so you could faintly see the model behind it.

Figure 7-41
West Elevation typical for each side of the house.

West Elevation Layer Organization

Layer	Contents	Scale
Dimensions	Dimensions, annotations	N/A
Models2	-	-
Models	**E1_West**	1/4" = 1'-0"
TitleBlock	Titleblock elements	N/A

Floor Height Notation

On the elevation views, I placed dashed lines that indicate the height of each floor of the house. In order to accurately place the lines, I created some guides in SketchUp that I made visible by using a special scene. (**Figure 7-42**)

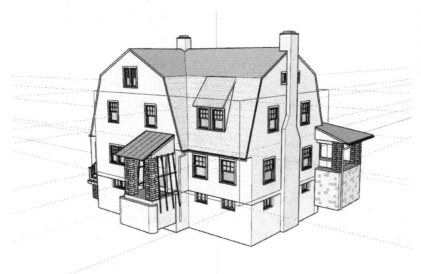

Figure 7-42
Guides are used to help place floor height notation in LayOut.

I added guides on each wall at the height of each floor. I then selected all of the guides and grouped them together. The group was then assigned to a special layer called **SP_guides**. I then created a scene that had that layer visible, along with most of the other layers.

The scene doesn't remember camera position so it allows me to switch viewports to it long enough for me to draw the dashed lines over the guides. Once I'm finished, I switch the viewport scene back to the originally intended scene.

Conclusion

Thank you for reading SketchUp to LayOut. You should now by able to tackle your next LayOut project with confidence. Use the various tricks you've learned to develop your own style and preferences as you continue to practice. With time I hope you'll agree that using SketchUp and LayOut together is fast, fun, and beautiful.

If you're interested in learning more about SketchUp and LayOut, go to my website at MasterSketchUp.com. You'll find dozens of free tutorials and videos to help you become a better modeler.

Video Course

As a follow up to this book, I've produced a video course that walks through all of the lessons of this book. To find out more, visit SketchUptoLayOut.com/videocourse.

Thank you,

Matt Donley

Matt@MasterSketchUp.com

Index